THE
GREAT COMPOSERS
THEIR LIVES AND TIMES

Johann Sebastian

Bach

1685-1750

Joseph

Haydn

1732-1809

Staff Credits

Editors
David Buxton BA (Honours)
Sue Lyon BA (Honours)

Art Editors
Debbie Jecock BA (Honours)
Ray Leaning BA (Honours),
PGCE (Art & Design)

Deputy Editor
Barbara Segall BA

Sub-editors
Geraldine Jones
Judy Oliver BA (Honours)
Nigel Rodgers BA (Honours), MA
Penny Smith
Will Steeds BA (Honours), MA

Designers
Steve Chilcott BA (Honours)
Shirin Patel BA (Honours)
Chris Rathbone

Picture Researchers
Georgina Barker
Julia Calloway BA (Honours)
Vanessa Cawley

Production Controllers
Sue Fuller
Steve Roberts

Secretary
Lynn Smail

Publisher
Terry Waters Grad IOP

Editorial Director
Maggi McCormick

Production Executive
Robert Paulley BSc

Managing Editor
Alan Ross BA (Honours)

Consultants
Dr Antony Hopkins
Commander of the Order
of the British Empire,
Fellow of the
Royal College of Music

Nick Mapstone BA (Honours), MA

Keith Shadwick BA (Honours)

Reference Edition Published 1987

Published by Marshall Cavendish Corporation
147 West Merrick Road
Freeport, Long Island
N.Y. 11520

Typeset by Walkergate Press Ltd, Hull, England
Printed and Bound in Singapore by
Koon Wah Printing Pte Ltd.

© Marshall Cavendish Limited MCMLXXXIV,
MCMLXXXVII

Library of Congress Cataloging-in-Publication Data

The Great composers, their lives and times.

Includes index.
1. Composers—Biography.   2. Music appreciation.
I. Marshall Cavendish Corporation.
ML390.G82   1987   780'.92'2 [B]   86-31294
ISBN 0-86307-776-5

ISBN 0-86307-776-5 (set)
     0-86307-781-1 (vol)

THE GREAT COMPOSERS
THEIR LIVES AND TIMES

Johann Sebastian

Bach

1685-1750

Joseph

Haydn

1732-1809

MARSHALL CAVENDISH
NEW YORK · LONDON · SYDNEY

THE
GREAT COMPOSERS
THEIR LIVES AND TIMES

Contents

Introduction

At first sight, Johann Sebastian Bach and Joseph Haydn seem very different; even their portraits (pages 7 and 87) show men of contrasting eras. With his full, curled wig, Bach is the epitome of the late Baroque, while Haydn is the true rational 18th-century gentleman. However, on closer examination, the two composers do have much in common. Like many composers, both Bach and Haydn came from musical families. The Bach's were a remarkable musical family and Bach passed on the family talent to his sons. Haydn's family was less obviously gifted, but his father, a wheelwright by trade, could play the harp without reading music (which suggests a natural talent) and recognized his son's ability.

Today both Bach and Haydn are of course regarded as great composers – Bach as the chief representative of the late Baroque, Haydn as the founder of the Viennese Classical school – and both were revered by their contemporaries. After their deaths, however, their fame declined: Bach's music was seen as old-fashioned, and Haydn's music was eclipsed by that of his younger contemporary, Mozart.

Although Bach's music was neglected by the public, the works of one of his sons, Carl Philipp Emanuel, greatly influenced later composers, including Haydn. C. P. E. Bach saw himself – and was regarded – as his father's true successor, saying that he never had any other teacher than his father for composition and keyboard playing. His Essay on the True Art of Playing Keyboard Instruments was said by Haydn to be the 'school of schools', and Haydn freely acknowledged his debt to Emanuel and through him, to his great father.

THE GREAT COMPOSERS

Johann Sebastian Bach

1685-1750

The Bach family was proud of its history of musical talent: in 1735 in his Ursprung der musicalisch Bachischen Familie, *Sebastian (many of the Bachs were named Johann, so it is usual to refer to them by the middle names) traced his family to Veit Bach, a baker who died in 1619. According to Sebastian, Veit used to play his cittern while grinding the corn and so learnt to keep musical time. In the late 18th century, Sebastian's sons, Christian and Emanuel, were seen as the greatest composers of the family, but today Sebastian is recognized as not only the greatest of the Bachs but also the foremost composer of the late Baroque and, with Mozart and Beethoven, stands at the summit of musical achievement. By analyzing and describing Bach's life and times, the following pages ensure that his music can be fully appreciated, admired and, not least, enjoyed.*

'Master of the Baroque'

In his own time, Bach was respected as a virtuoso organ player – now he is known and appreciated for the emotional depth of his Baroque music.

Ambrosius Bach (above), father of Johann Sebastian Bach, was a talented member of the musically gifted Bach family. In 1671 he became court trumpeter and director of music in Eisenach, where Bach was born in 1685. The portrait on the preceding page of Johann Sebastian Bach is one of only two existing authentic likenesses of the composer.

Johann Sebastian Bach was born in 1685 in Eisenach, Thuringia (in what is now East Germany), into a family firmly established locally as a musical one; it is reported that in some parts of Thuringia, the very word 'Bach' had come to denote a 'musician'.

Ambrosius Bach of Eisenach, Johann Sebastian's father, was a good violinist and trumpeter. From 1671 he was court trumpeter and director of town music in Eisenach.

By the time Sebastian was ten both parents had died and he was adopted by his eldest brother Christoph, organist of the Michaeliskirche in Ohrdruf, a small town near to Eisenach. Christoph was a skilled organist and Sebastian praised him as 'a profound composer'. Since no works by Christoph are known, Bach probably meant that he was a creative keyboard improviser. Certainly Christoph Bach exerted a profound influence on Sebastian. He taught him to play keyboard instruments and introduced him to the technique needed in music-copying. During this time Sebastian gained practical experience in organ-building, since the main Michaeliskirche organ was substantially repaired under Christoph's supervision.

Education in Lüneberg

By the time Bach was 15 accommodation in his brother's home was at a premium. His brother had two children and a third on the way; so Bach left the house to take up a chorister-scholarship at the Michaelisschule, in Lüneberg.

At Lüneberg, Bach became a member of the Mettenchor (Matins Choir). Members of this choir were usually boys from poor families. They received free schooling, board and lodgings and were paid a small amount depending on their seniority. They also received a share in fees for weddings and other

special occasions they took part in.

Bach sang in the choir until his voice broke, changing from a treble to a bass baritone, then he became an instrumentalist. At school he studied Latin, Lutheranism, arithmetic, history and geography, German poetry, physics, heraldry and genealogy.

While he was at Lüneberg he heard the organist of the Johanniskirche, Georg Böhm, play. Böhm probably advised Bach to hear Adam Reincken, the distinguished organist of the Hamburg Catharinenkirche. Bach was impressed by both Reincken's showy playing and the church's organ itself.

From 1702, aged 17, Bach was on his own. In March 1703, after a few unsuccessful attempts to find work, he was employed at a minor Weimar court as a musician, but was paid as a 'lackey'.

Bach was 15 when he became a chorister-scholar at the Michaelisschule, the school associated with the Michaeliskirche (above left).

While a student, Bach went to Hamburg to hear J. A. Reincken (above), the organist of the Catharinenkirche.

Bach spent nine years in Weimar (left) as a court musician.

In August 1703, he was appointed organist of the new Church in Arnstadt. In fact, the young Bach had first been approached by the church committee (the Consistory) of Arnstadt to examine the newly repaired organ earlier in 1703. He so distinguished himself that the church committtee offered him the job, over the head of a local man, Andreas Börner.

In Arnstadt, Bach's duties were comparatively light, but their specific nature was never clearly established, and later this gave rise to disputes. Bach had an excitable temperament and failed to gain the confidence of the local student musicians. He also irritated the Consistory which had so generously urged his appointment, and was unpopular with his congregation. He was most roundly censured for extending approved leave from four weeks to nearly three months and, as a result, for leaving his assistant to play for Advent and Christmas 1705 and the New Year festivities of 1706. The Consistory found his explanation unsatisfactory, and they also complained that his accompaniments to chorales were too involved for ordinary congregational singing. There was also a complaint from the Consistory about the presence of a 'stranger maiden' in the organ gallery. However, this was his future wife, and he had permission for her presence from the parson.

The reason for his absence around Advent and Christmas can only have been for one purpose: to attend the celebrated evening sacred concerts (*Abendmusiken*) of Lübeck's Jacobikirche, organized by the famous Danish master-organist and composer Dietrich Buxtehude.

In midsummer 1707, Bach left Arnstadt to take up an appointment as organist of the Blasiuskirche in Mühlhausen. Despite the brevity of his stay in Mühlhausen – just over a year – it was an eventful time. He wrote his first cantatas as well as many works for the town council. It was also in Mühlhausen that he married his first wife, Maria Barbara Bach, a distant cousin and, like Sebastian himself, the child of a musical member of the Bach family. They had met while he was in Arnstadt, and were married in her home village of Dornheim in 1707.

Bach left Mühlhausen in 1708 to take up an appointment at the court of the Duke of Weimar.

Konzertmeister in Weimar

This offer of engagement – voiced as a command – had been issued by Duke Wilhelm Ernst of Saxe-Weimar, one of Thuringia's most important noblemen, whose court was of important cultural and theological standing. Bach worked under his patronage in Weimar from July 1708 to December 1717. At first he was court organist but from 2 March 1714 he was invested with the newly created title of *Konzertmeister*. In Weimar, Bach composed a large quantity of organ music, his harpsichord toccatas and a strikingly expressive series of cantatas for the Ducal chapel. One of his commissions, a birthday cantata for the pretentious Duke Christian of Weissenfels, marked the start of an association with the Weissenfels court which lasted until that Duke's death and the end of his line in 1736.

During his Weimar period, six of his children were born. Bach and his wife kept touch with friends and relations from Ohrdruf, Arnstadt and Mühlhausen by making them godparents to their children.

Bach's skill attracted students and from this time onwards he was never without pupils. He was offered an important organist's post at Halle when

Bach often travelled great distances to hear famous musicians perform. One of his more epic journeys was in the winter of 1705, when he walked from Arnstadt to Lübeck to hear the Danish organist Dietrich Buxtehude. He is thought to have attended a series of evening recitals, including one where the Castrum doloris *(below) was performed. Bach overstayed his four weeks' leave and when he returned to Arnstadt three months later, was reprimanded by the church committee.*

Handel's teacher, Zachow died. He did not take up the post because, when he asked permission to leave Weimar, the Duke created him Konzertmeister, and the employers at Halle could not match the salary which went with his new post. His relationship with Halle remained good and in 1717 he was praised in print as 'the famous Weimar organist', by the influential Hamburg composer, Mattheson.

Particularly significant to 18th-century musicians was his visit to the Saxon capital city of Dresden late in 1717, where a contest was arranged by an influential nobleman. Bach and the great French keyboard-player and composer, Louis Marchand, were invited to play (and presumably to extemporize) in a harpsichord competition. There are various accounts of this event, or non-event, as it turned out, since Marchand quit Dresden leaving Bach without an opponent. This was taken by many, then and later, to be a sure sign of the 'superiority' of German music over French.

A sour note at Weimar

Although his first years at Weimar had been creative, the last year of his employment there was disagreeable. Family feuds in Weimar's royal house and the unsavoury manipulation to find a new Kapellmeister were the causes of his dissatisfaction. As a result Bach decided to look elsewhere for a position as Kapellmeister. An offer came from Prince Leopold of Anhalt-Cöthen, so Bach sought his release again from Duke Wilhelm, and was again refused. When Bach again asked permission to go, the Duke placed him under house arrest from 6 November 1717 and then dismissed him in disgrace on 2 December.

Kapellmeister to Prince Leopold

Relations with his new employer were good. Prince Leopold was a musical young man and he gave Bach every encouragement to write all kinds of instrumental and secular vocal music.

In Cöthen, the last of Bach's children by his first wife was born, a son, named after Prince Leopold, who was his godfather. Sadly, the child did not live for very long.

Unlike most of the un-authentic portraits of Bach, this one (right), depicts him as a young Konzertmeister at the court of the Duke of Weimar in 1715.

Despite this sadness, Bach later wrote that in Cöthen he was generally very happy. He apparently composed very fluently here: to this period belong the sonatas for violin and harpsichord, the unaccompanied solos for violin and for cello, and the *Six Concertos* which we know as the 'Brandenburg' Concertos. The first book of the *Well-Tempered Clavier* and a number of vocal works written to honour the Prince's birthday and to express devotion to him at the opening of each new year date from this time in Cöthen.

However, from 1720–21, Bach suffered a series of setbacks. While he was away attending, with other musicians, the visit of the Prince to the spa at Karlsbad his wife, Maria Barbara, died.

Second, he failed to take up the post of organist of the Jacobikirche in Hamburg, either because he was

A Kantor (below left) directs a group of music students. In German cities, from the Reformation until the mid-18th century, this was a highly sought-after post. As Kantor of the Thomaskirche and Thomasschule (below) in Leipzig, from 1723 until his death in 1750, Bach was director of church and school music. Mendelssohn's sketch shows the Bach Memorial – which he donated – in the centre foreground.

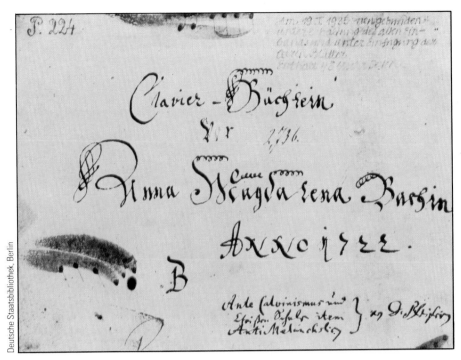

One of many music albums Bach made for members of his family, the Clavier-Büchlein (above) is dedicated to his second wife, Anna Magdalena. It contains some first drafts of Bach's compositions and some by his children.

involved him in no little expense. In any event, by March 1721 Bach was clearly angling for offers of employment elsewhere.

In December 1721 Bach married Anna Magdalena Wilken. Like Bach she was the child of a *Hoftrompeter* (Chief Trumpeter) and was herself a professional singer. She may also have wished him to move, but this is uncertain.

The mature years in Leipzig

As Kantor of the Thomasschule, Bach held one of the most important music posts in Lutheran Europe: only Kantor of Hamburg ranked higher. Bach was the town's most important musician, responsible for the music of four Leipzig churches and for any music which might be required for civic functions. The musical training of students at the school attached to Thomaskirche was also his responsibility. His main church duties extended to music for the principal services and feasts, as well as weddings and funerals, for which he received separate fees. He received a salary and payments in kind, of corn and wine, and was housed in the newly-renovated south wing of the Thomasschule. His first six years in Leipzig were demonstrably the most productive of his busy life. Until 1726, he composed elaborate music for his first choir. This was made up of the 12–16 best singers and was directed by Bach himself.

In 1728, he once again found himself in dispute with the church authorities; this time over the question of who should choose the songs to be sung before and after vespers. From this time his dealings with both council members and teachers at the Thomasschule were difficult. It seems that when confronted with what he saw as undue pressure, Bach reacted defiantly against the bureaucracy.

In 1729, after spending some time away from

unwilling or unable to donate to church funds the vast sum expected from successful candidates. So, the last chance he had of becoming the regular player of a really outstanding instrument of this kind passed out of his hands.

The third setback was the remarriage of Leopold on 11 December 1721 to his cousin, Princess Friderica of Anhalt-Bernburg, a lady who was not in any way artistically inclined. Possibly she was jealous of her husband's former love of music – which had

An imaginative 19th-century representation of the Bach family (right). It shows Bach at the keyboard, and other members of the family playing and singing. Bach married twice and had 20 children, but only 9 of them survived to mature ages. All the children received musical training from Bach and in 1730 he was proud to report that he could form a vocal and instrumental ensemble with his family. Three of his sons, Wilhelm Friedeman, Carl Philip Emanuel and Johann Christian, became composers.

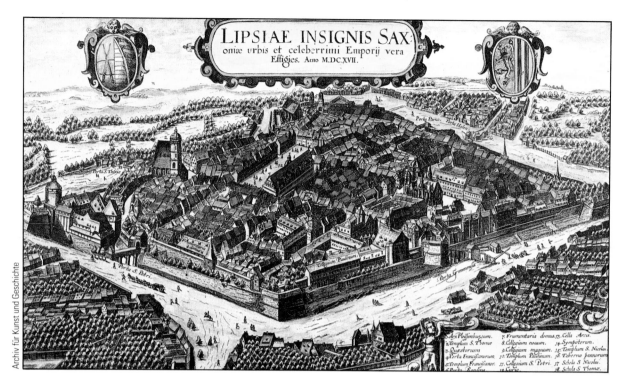

Leipzig at the Weissenfels court, he was given the title of court Kapellmeister of Saxe-Weissenfels. During this year he also returned to Cöthen to perform funeral music on the death of his former employer, Prince Leopold.

On his return to Leipzig he became director of the collegium musicum which had been founded by Telemann in 1704. This was a loose association of musicans and students which gave weekly public concerts. This gave him the opportunity for writing more secular music more declamatory in its style. His works were scaled for the larger numbers now at his disposal.

Although he was writing less sacred music his interest was as strong as ever and most of his major ecclesiastical works were written after 1730. Throughout his Leipzig period he provided performances of his cantatas every Sunday, and in 1731 the first performance of the *St Mark Passion* took place on Good Friday.

During a five-month period of national mourning on the death of Elector Friedrich August I of Saxony in 1733, Bach began writing the Kyrie and Gloria of his B minor Mass. Hoping that this would be the means of a new appointment at court, he presented them to the new Elector Friedrich August II in Dresden. They were probably performed at the Sophienkirche where his son, W. F. Bach, was working as organist, but the only title given to him was that of *Hofkomponist*.

In 1737 Bach resigned from the directorship of the collegium musicum and turned to keyboard music, working on the *Well-Tempered Clavier* and the third part of the *Clavier-Übung*. He probably also devoted more time to private teaching.

Bach once again took over as director of the collegium musicum in 1739, but withdrew in 1741 when Gottfried Zimmermann, the coffee-house owner in whose premises the collegium performed, died. In August 1741 Bach journeyed to Berlin to see his son, C. P. E. Bach, who in 1738 had been appointed court harpsichord player to Crown Prince Frederick of Prussia (Frederick the Great). He also

visited Dresden where he presented a copy of the Aria with 30 variations to Count von Keyserlingk for use by his resident harpsichord player Johann Gottlieb Goldberg. These were the 'Goldberg' variations.

From 1742 Bach composed only a few sacred cantatas and the *Peasant Cantata* of 1742 was his last secular work. He concentrated on performances of his major works and of those of other composers, such as Telemann and Handel. He also kept up his interest in organ building and examined and inaugurated many church organs.

In 1747, through Count von Keyserlingk he received an invitation to visit the court of Frederick the Great. He began his visit with a piano exercise in fugal improvisation on a theme given by the king. There followed on the next day an organ recital and chamber music recital where Bach again improvised.

On his return to Leipzig he began writing down and working on the King of Prussia's fugue theme. He turned this into a larger work, the 'Musical Offering', dedicated to Frederick which was printed in September 1747.

During his declining years, Bach struggled with failing eyesight. In 1749 an English eye specialist, John Taylor, performed an operation on him which was partly successful and a second operation left him very weak. Nevertheless in May 1750 he took on a last pupil, Johann Gottfried Müthel, but it is uncertain how much he was actually able to instruct him.

He received his last Communion on 22 July and died on 28 July 1750 at home, after a stroke. His second wife survived him by ten years, then died in poverty. Bach had left a modest estate, all of which was divided between his widow and the nine surviving children of both marriages.

Before he died, his music had become unfashionable, and for 50 years after his death nothing of his was published. However, later both Mozart and Beethoven found much to be admired in his music, but it was through Mendelssohn (from 1829) that Bach's works were once again revived.

Bach spent 27 years in Leipzig (above), as Kantor of the Thomaskirche and Director of Music of Leipzig. This was the most productive period of his life and he composed huge quantities of sacred music, including 6 cycles of cantatas – about 300 cantatas in all. As Director of the collegium musicum, he had the opportunity to produce music of a less religious nature. His great Passions, the St Matthew and St John Passions, were first performed in Leipzig and between Christmas Day 1734 and Epiphany 1735, the Christmas Oratorio was first heard.

'A most musical family'

Today the name Bach conjures up the glorious music of Johann Sebastian Bach – yet during his life and long after his death his sons' music outshone his own.

Photo Jörg P. Anders

By the time Johann Sebastian Bach was born in 1685, there were already fourteen professional musicians in the Bach family and a further ten children under the age of 15 who would eventually follow the same vocation. The family's association with music began with Sebastian's great grandfather Johannes, born in 1550, and continued until the death of Sebastian's grandson, Wilhelm Friedrich Ernst Bach in 1845. Throughout this period, the family held a pre-eminent position in local musical life in the central region of Germany where they lived. Many of the local musical posts in churches, towns and courts were held by members of the Bach family and in many instances, son succeeded father and was later succeeded by his own son, cousin or nephew.

The musical association was further strengthened by intermarriage with other musical families in the area, such as the Wilckes, Lämmerhirts and the Hoffmanns. Sebastian followed the family tradition in this respect: his first wife was a Bach – a distant cousin – and his second a Wilckes. This intense interest in music created a close unity within the family, and the regular family gatherings must at times have resembled a musical festival, with everyone joining in.

The portait above is thought to be one of only three authentic likenesses of Bach. Here, he is shown on the left, with Gottfried Heinrich, the first son of his second marriage and the two eldest sons of his first marriage, Carl Philipp Emanuel and Wilhelm Friedemann.

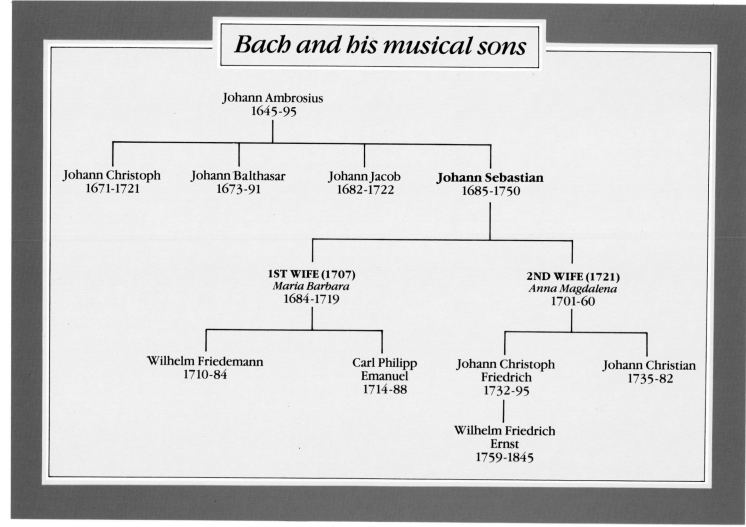

Bach and his musical sons

Johann Ambrosius
1645-95

Johann Christoph
1671-1721

Johann Balthasar
1673-91

Johann Jacob
1682-1722

Johann Sebastian
1685-1750

1ST WIFE (1707)
Maria Barbara
1684-1719

2ND WIFE (1721)
Anna Magdalena
1701-60

Wilhelm Friedemann
1710-84

Carl Philipp
Emanuel
1714-88

Johann Christoph
Friedrich
1732-95

Johann Christian
1735-82

Wilhelm Friedrich
Ernst
1759-1845

Part of the Bach family tree showing the line from Bach's father, Ambrosius, through to Bach's grandson, Wilhelm Friedrich. In 1843 Wilhelm Friedrich, the only surviving grandson, was guest of honour at the unveiling of the Bach Memorial in front of the Thomasschule in Leipzig.

The western outskirts of Leipzig (right) from the back of the house where Bach lived as Kantor of Leipzig for 27 years. It was in this house that many of his younger relatives stayed either as his pupils or as tutors for his sons.

The earlier members of the Bach family excelled principally as performers rather than composers, but it would be wrong to imply that they were not creative musicians. During the 17th century, spontaneity was an important part of the art of performance. Organists in Germany had to improvise upon the hymns or chorales of the Lutheran church, and players of melody instruments, violinists and wind players, were expected to interpret freely any written lines, when playing for dancing and other occasions. The creativity of the early Bachs was, therefore, of a more immediate nature, and Sebastian's father, Johann Ambrosius Bach, seems to have been particularly skilled in this art of supplying an instant answer on musical occasions.

Much of what we do know about the early Bachs comes to us through Sebastian's interest in his musical forbears. Quite early in his life, he came into possession of a collection of music begun by his father, Johann Ambrosius, and entitled the *Alt-Bachischies Archiv* (Archive of the old Bachs). This included examples of several different styles of sacred choral music written by earlier members of the family. This collection was destroyed during World War II, but its contents had already been partly preserved in a modern edition made by Max Schneider in 1935. A historical manuscript started by Sebastian and continued by his son Carl Philipp Emanuel Bach entitled *Ursprung der musicalisch-Bachischen Familie, 1735* has also been lost, but this

Alexander Thiele 'View of Leipzig' Museum für Geschichte der Stadt Leipzig

Staatliche Galerie Moritzburg Halle

Wilhelm Friedemann Bach (above), reported to be Bach's favourite son, was from an early age a talented keyboard player. Bach himself was his teacher in clavier and organ playing and in composition. From 1746–1764 he was organist at the Halle Liebfrauenkirche (right), holding the same post that Bach had applied for in 1713.

Archiv für Kunst und Geschichte

too, is preserved in print. This manuscript was an attempt to trace the origins of the musical Bach family, and though it failed to do this satisfactorily, it did give excellent summaries of the life and work of many of the Bachs active in the late 17th and early 18th centuries.

Johann Ambrosius Bach

Sebastian's father, Johann Ambrosius Bach, was born in Erfurt in 1645, and received his musical training both in Erfurt and Arnstadt from his father, Christoph Bach. Christoph was a violinist who worked in the town bands of both towns and was also employed in the then flourishing ducal household in the beautiful, historical town of Arnstadt.

After starting his career alongside his father in Arnstadt, Ambrosius moved to Erfurt where he served under the direction of his cousin Johann Christian Bach in the city's municipal ensemble. Ambrosius also worked in Erfurt as a violinist but, like his father, later left for Eisenach where he served both the town and the local nobility. Here, in 1671, he became both Court Trumpeter and director of the town's music.

In his new post, he showed unusual talent – in 1772, the Eisenach town chronicle reported that he organized the music for Easter 'with organ, violins, voices, trumpets and kettledrums, something which had never previously been known in Eisenach's history'. Ambrosius's portrait, painted in Eisenach, gives him a robust and a genial appearance. He was valued and sought after as a musical director, and he passed on qualities of dedication and musical enterprise to his three surviving sons, Johann Christoph, Johann Jacob and Johann Sebastian.

During his lifetime, Sebastian worked in close association with many of his lesser-known cousins and other relatives. These included two slightly older contemporaries – Johann Bernhard and Johann Ludwig – whose music he promoted and performed in Leipzig. Sebastian's younger contemporaries were often given lodging and training by their distinguished elder cousin. Some, like his nephew Johann Bernhard from Ohrdruf, seem to have served a longish unofficial apprenticeship with him. Indeed, Bernhard stayed in the Bach households at Weimar and Köthen for four years – between 1715 and 1719. Others lodged in the Kantor's quarter of the Thomasschule in Leipzig while they were attached to the university. One of these, Johann Elias Bach from Schweinfurt, studied theology in Leipzig from 1738 to 1742 and in return for his board and lodging, he acted as tutor to Sebastian's younger children and assisted the busy composer by writing letters for him and making copies of these.

A number of younger Bachs were awarded boarding scholarships at St Thomas's between 1723 and 1750, and almost certainly they were carefully trained under the watchful eye of Sebastian and his older sons. In fact, the Bach family continued to flourish throughout central Germany until well after Sebastian's death, independently of the important positions reached by his own sons. The tradition the lesser Bachs continued to foster was that established by their ancestors – they produced tailor-made musical work in different artistic areas. It is through the work of some of these less compelling members of the clan that much of the magnificent music for keyboard of Johann Sebastian Bach and his predecessors has been preserved for posterity in collected albums of manuscripts.

Carl Philipp Emanuel (above), Bach's second son, was not only a talented and successful musician but he was also the careful guardian for posterity of his father's musical legacy.

Emanuel worked in both Berlin and Hamburg for a large part of his life and attracted a large circle of literary and artistic friends. He is shown right with two such friends – the artist A. Stöttrup and Pastor Sturm. Sturm, a devout evangelist, wrote a number of religious poems which Emanuel set to music and published in 1780 and 1781.

Sebastian's sons

It was, in fact, through the work of Sebastian's sons that the family became most celebrated internationally. In their music, it is apparent for the first time that as well as following fashion the Bach family also took the lead in setting style. Sebastian's music has been seen, with hindsight, to be profoundly original and its influence on composers of the Romantic and Modern eras has been immense.

By his two marriages, Bach had six sons who survived into adulthood. All were bound to be musical given the family background but around 1780, references to 'the music of Bach' meant that of his second son Carl Philipp Emanuel, throughout most of Germany, and that of his youngest son Johann Christian, to the English. The years between about 1755 and 1775 witnessed the progressive eclipse of Sebastian's fame behind the rising international reputation of these two sons, together with the varying fame and fortunes enjoyed by their elder brothers, Wilhelm Friedemann and Johann Christoph Friedrich.

The two middle sons, Johann Gottfried Bernhard and Gottfried Heinrich, were also musical but little is known of their lives and their careers probably because Johann Gottfried Bernhard was short-lived – he died aged 24 – and Gottfried Heinrich became simple-minded at the onset of puberty.

Wilhelm Friedemann Bach

Wilhelm Friedemann was the first son born to Sebastian and his first wife, Maria Barbara Bach. He was talented as a keyboard player from a young age, and for a time at the age of 15 was sent from Leipzig to the great Johann Gottlieb Graun in Merseburg for violin lessons. Friedemann excelled as an organist, and his first two posts, at the Dresden Sophienkirche and the Halle Liebfrauenkirche, must have seemed full of promise to his ageing father, who had started life in far less exalted positions in Arnstadt and Mühlhausen. Neither of these cities had an instrument that was remotely comparable to the excellent new Silbermann organ in Dresden or the Reichel and Contius organs of the Halle Church. However, Friedemann, who is reported to have been his father's favourite son, never really fulfilled his

Johann Christoph Friedrich Bach (above) was the first son of Bach's second marriage. He spent most of his working life in the service of the Counts of Schaumburg-Lippe in Bückeberg.

In 1738 Carl Philipp Emanuel moved from Frankfurt-on-Oder to Berlin (above). Soon after this move he was appointed 'Accompagnist' to the Prussian Crown Prince at the nearby court of Rheinsberg. When the Crown Prince succeeded to the Prussian throne in 1740 as Frederick II, Carl Philipp Emanuel returned with him to Berlin. Here he married the daughter of a wine merchant and made a name for himself as a composer. He remained in the King's service until 1767 when he was offered the post of director of music in Hamburg.

early promise. His career was dogged by ill-fortune, including severe poverty, restlessness and dissatisfaction with his situation, and after his father's death, he was gradually forced to depend solely upon his abilities as a keyboard teacher to support himself. In 1770, he was forced to move to Brunswick and four years later to Berlin. In Berlin he was welcomed by supporters who had known his father and his brother Emanuel. Among these were the Princess Anna Amalia (sister of Frederick the Great), her court composer and librarian Johann Philipp Kirnberger (a former pupil and staunch admirer of Sebastian) and probably also the Nikolaikirche Kantor, Johann Georg Lehmann. However, his habit of mistrusting others and behaving less than admirably towards his rivals resulted in enmity between Friedemann and Kirnberger, and when he died in July 1784 he was poor and little-known.

Friedemann's music was composed to suit the places where he worked. In fashionable Dresden, he composed mainly elegant ensemble music. In Halle he arranged and composed a number of weighty choral compositions for the church, besides a quantity of keyboard music for teaching purposes – especially from 1764 when he ungraciously withdrew from his post at the Liebfrauenkirche. His *12 Polonaises* of this period show him to be a composer of some stature and versatility, capable of writing tenderly, brilliantly and emphatically by turns.

In Berlin, he continued to concentrate mainly on keyboard music, publishing eight fugues and attempting a modern dramatic style in sonatas and smaller pieces. His music never lacks individual character, although its ingredients are clearly derived from others, but in longer structures there is a lack of proportion, seen by some as reflecting the style of his life.

Carl Philipp Emanuel Bach

Carl Philipp Emanuel Bach was born to Maria Barbara Bach in 1714, when his father was 28. After studies in Köthen and as a day-pupil of the Leipzig Thomasschule, he entered Leipzig University as a law student in 1731. Law was then a rather broader subject than that referred to today, and denoted a practical interest in what is now called the 'liberal arts' or 'humanities'. This may have prompted him to broaden his outlook and seek his fortune further afield than Leipzig as, in 1734, his name was recorded on the registers of the University of Frankfurt-on-Oder, situated near the Polish border.

Emanuel was left-handed, and in his autobiography claims that this prevented him from playing stringed instruments as a young man. As a result, he seems briefly to have taken up the flute – a very fashionable instrument in the 1730s – before devoting all of his attention to mastering keyboard instruments. These included the organ, the harpsichord and the clavichord, and on the latter, he was probably the most expert virtuoso of all time. Accounts of his playing describe how, when improvising, he became 'as a man possessed'. Yet he was cool and purposeful enough to be able to read his father's music at sight, and to be able to accompany the scrupulous and quixotic King Frederick the Great at sight.

Emanuel's music also contains many contrasts. At times it is very exciting and dramatic, with chords and scales succeeding one another in such rapid succession that the effect is almost overwhelming. At others, it is so emotionally intense as to be almost unbearable. However, behind the emotion lies a sense of purpose and of controlled power that has led to Emanuel's music being compared to Beethoven's, (who, in fact, expressed great admiration for it).

Emanuel's career was the most impressive of all

In May 1762 Johann Christian Bach left Milan for England where he stayed for the rest of his life. He shared lodgings for a time with his friend and compatriot Carl Friedrich Abel, a composer and viola da gamba player. For many years they held successful series of joint concerts. In 1774 they acquired a property on the corner of Hanover Street and Hanover Square (below). A new concert hall – the Hanover Square Rooms – was built in the garden and here in 1775 they gave the first in a new series of Bach–Abel concerts. The project was not a financial success and competition from a series of concerts at the Pantheon led to a decline in popularity of the Bach–Abel concerts.

the Bachs. From 1738 to March 1768 he was in the service of Frederick, who was at first Crown Prince, and later King of Prussia. Despite his instability of temperament, Frederick was the model for the historians' notion of 'enlightened despotism'. Working daily for the flute-playing King as his accompanist for a rather meagre salary was not always an agreeable task, but it did place Emanuel in a prominent position at the centre of a powerful government. It also gave him the opportunity to work alongside colleagues of the highest order – the brothers Graun and Benda, the flute-teacher Quantz and a fully professional opera company. His position also enabled him to find rich pupils easily, and as a system of alternating with a second harpsichordist operated for accompanying the King at chamber-music evenings he had free time in which to compose and to teach. In the 1740s, Emanuel was already composing pieces which pointed forwards in either style or structure towards the music of Mozart and Beethoven. Before he left Berlin he had composed a wealth of elegant music.

In 1768, Emanuel succeeded his godfather, Georg Philipp Telemann, as Director of Church Music in the city of Hamburg. This was one of the most important posts in European church music. There were five churches under his control, and there were huge numbers of incidental tasks connected with the almost unceasing round of festivals attached to the

various merchant trades of the prosperous trading port. Emanuel, who seems to have inherited the larger part of Sebastian's combination of industry and practicality, fulfilled these demanding requirements with distinction, and also found time to compose as much music as his predecessor. He published sets of his own works, promoted the music of others and revised and republished one of the most important textbooks of instrumental music ever written, his *Essay on the true art of playing keyboard instruments,* published in Berlin in 1753. By the time of his death in 1788 he was considered to be the father of North European music and had gained a great international reputation as a musician.

Johann Christoph Friedrich Bach
Johann Christoph Friedrich Bach was the first child of Anna Magdalena, Sebastian's second wife. He spent his life in reasonably steady employment in the service of the Counts Wilhelm and Philipp Ernst of Schaumburg-Lippe in Bückeburg. He secured his first post – as a chamber-musician – on Sebastian's recommendation in early 1750 and remained at Bückeburg until his death in 1795.

Friedrich is reported to have been an excellent harpsichordist, but his chief successes as a composer were in vocal music. He apparently acquired a taste for this from his Italian superiors and was further encouraged by the presence of an excellent literary

Soon after he arrived in England Johann Christian Bach was engaged as music master to the German-speaking Queen Charlotte (above), and through her patronage obtained a privilege for the publication of his works.

Thomas Gainsborough 'J. C. Bach'. Liceo Musicale, Bologna/Archiv für Kunst und Geschichte

Johann Christian Bach (left) one of the most versatile composers of the late 18th century, was the most important influence on the young Mozart who visited him in London.

collaborator, Johann Gottfried Herder who was in Bückeburg from 1771 to 1776. A visit to his younger brother, Johann Christian, in London in the winter of 1778–79 also provided him with an opportunity to familiarize himself with the new Italian-influenced classic style of Mozart, and soon after his return, he organized performances of Mozart's *Il Seraglio* and Gluck's *Iphigenie en Tauride* in Bückeburg.

As a composer, Friedrich was tasteful rather than dramatically original, and it was in his cantatas (especially their recitatives) and his oratorios that his sense of propriety resulted in music of real quality. Towards the end of his life, he became influenced by the warm symphonic style of his younger brother Christian and of Mozart.

Johann Christian Bach

Johann Christian Bach, Sebastian's youngest child, lived a far less commendable life than his brother Friedrich, yet he too was a composer of great international significance. At his father's death he was briefly adopted by Emanuel, and went to live with him in Berlin. In 1754, however, he set off for Italy, where he studied with Mozart's teacher in Bologna – Padre Martini – visited Naples and eventually settled in Milan. There, he secured an appointment as one of the two cathedral organists in 1760 – at some stage in the late 1750s, he became a Roman Catholic.

In Italy, he enjoyed several liaisons with operatic singers and eventually married one of them in 1773. These liaisons would probably have distressed his father had he lived to hear of them, and would probably not have pleased his brothers either. However, his captivation with female singers was secondary to his falling in love with Italian opera, and it was in this genre that he was to work most enthusiastically for the rest of his life.

During his early Italian years, Christian wrote some accomplished religious choral works, including a *Requiem* and a *Dixit Dominus,* but from 1760 he turned his attention to the stage. After *Artaserse* which was performed in Turin in 1760, he achieved a notable success with *Catone in Utica.* His success led to offers of work in Venice and London. In May 1762, he left Milan for England which was to become home for the rest of his lfe. On arriving in London, the young Bach soon established himself as an accomplished opera-composer and director and eventually became known as 'the London Bach'. He also secured an engagement as music teacher to the German-speaking Queen Charlotte and this appointment led to useful privileges which resulted in the publication of keyboard concertos and other works. From 1765, he shared lodgings, and the direction of a very important series of public concerts, with Carl Friedrich Abel – a brilliant virtuoso on the viola da gamba; Abel's own father had worked under Sebastian in Köthen half a century earlier.

In April 1764, the young Wolfgang Mozart arrived in London in the company of his father Leopold. They stayed in London for about 14 months during which time a spontaneous bond of affection sprang up between Wolfgang and Christian. The extremely gracious charm of Christian's Italianate style must have appealed strongly to the young Mozart, for he readily adopted many of its characteristics and mannerisms, making them more and more his own in the ensuing years. Mozart learned more than stylistic mannerisms from Christian, however, and there is clear evidence in both Mozart's early keyboard concertos and in his subsequent symphonies that he was interested also in the structures and techniques of Christian's music.

Like most operatic composers who have worked in London's commercial theatres, Christian Bach did not achieve consistent success, nor did he earn regular financial returns. However, things generally went well until after 1778, the year he played host to his brother Friedrich and his nephew Wilhelm Friedrich Ernst Bach, the last of Sebastian's musical descendants. His popularity with the fickle London concert public began to wane, and he was already in debt before a mischievous housekeeper defrauded him of over £1000, leaving him to end his life in depressing circumstances.

Yet at the height of his fame around 1770, Christian was in great demand as a composer of opera. In 1772 and 1774 he wrote commissioned pieces for the Mannheim Court – then the musical centre of Europe. In 1797 he composed *Amadis de Gaule,* a French opera for Paris, based on a much earlier libretto by Quinault, and his London compositions occasionally found their way into European theatres. However, the international interest aroused by the publication of his instrumental music was probably of even greater significance. His musical language appealed strongly to ears accustomed to appropriately tasteful music. Most of his music was not very hard to play, it was tuneful, and it was exactly suited to the essentially pretty sounds of contemporary instruments. Many of the Bachs had regularly produced more stirring stuff than Christian ever did, but only rarely, when at their very best, excelled him in music that was so compellingly attractive and lovable.

COMPOSER'S LIFE

Bach and the Church

For over a hundred years, Germany was torn apart by conflict between the Protestant (Lutheran) and Roman Catholic Churches. This struggle was embittered by political wars between the Holy Roman Emperor and the German princes, and was ended only by the Treaty of Westphalia in 1648. The treaty established religious toleration for both Protestants and Catholics and by the time Bach was born, the spirit of toleration was well-established in Germany. Although the spirit of the age was increasingly secular, Bach – like most of his contemporaries – was a deeply religious man, and the Lutheran chorale and church organ music were major influences on his musical output. However, Bach also drew on contemporary French and Italian styles to form a near-perfect synthesis of traditional and contemporary music for the Lutheran Church.

COMPOSER'S LIFE
'God is my King'

Although the Protestant Church in Germany was divided between the differing views of Lutheranism and Pietism, Bach wrote church music as an expression of his own religious feelings – a blend of the two.

Bach's religious feelings grew in the new climate of religious toleration which evolved in the aftermath of the bitter Thirty Years' War (below) – a dynastic struggle focused on Germany which developed into a collision between the Catholic and Protestant Churches.

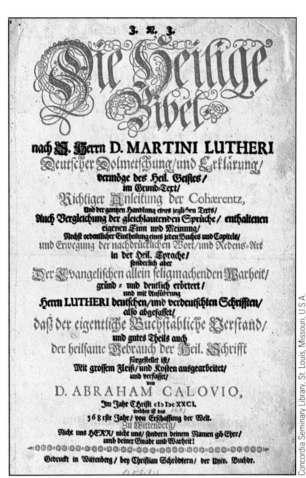

Martin Luther (far left) a German religious reformer, whose 'protestant' doctrines were the basis for Bach's religious upbringing.

The title page (left) of the Calov Bible, one of the many religious books in Bach's library. This edition of Luther's translation of the Bible was published in 1681 in three folio volumes with a commentary by the publisher, the Wittenberg professor of theology, Abraham Calov. Calov was one of the most prominent representatives of Lutheran high orthodoxy.

In many parts of Europe, only a century before Bach's birth in 1685, to reject the Catholic religion was to invite torture and even public execution. The power of the church was such that religion almost dominated everyday life. But during the following century – at least in northern Europe – matters changed rapidly and radically. Automatic allegiance to the Catholic Church, or to Catholic rulers, was brought into question by an increasing tide of 'unorthodox' religious feeling which shook the supremacy of catholicism. After 1530 and the early Reformation in Germany, protestantism as pioneered by Martin Luther took root in many parts of Europe. But the development of differing religious identities of the nations of Europe was not easily won and gradually led to open hostility culminating with the conflict known as the Thirty Years' War (1618–1648). In essence this was a struggle for the balance of power between the Austrian Hapsburgs and the German Princes. Germany, then a collection of separate states, was divided by religious factionalism as well as dynastic rivalries and became the focal point of the long, drawn-out and debilitating war.

The depredations of this conflict left most of Germany in ruins. Only after peace was signed in Westphalia in 1648 could people anywhere in Europe look forward with any degree of optimism to a future where religious differences might not assume such great proportions.

Lutherans and Pietists

By the time Bach was born religious toleration was the order of the day. A new, more worldly and material, rather than spiritual, outlook was apparent in all aspects of life. Although music too, was freed from specific church use, many composers like Bach wrote both sacred and secular music with equal interest and enthusiasm. Bach was a deeply religious man and he expressed this in his music; nevertheless, in retrospect, his music can be seen as part of this general process of secularization.

Germany in the late 17th century was made up of over 300 little states, each with its own autocratic ruler and court, and each subscribing also to a church. In most of Germany that church was protestant, although by now it had divided into several denominations within the Protestant Church. In the north, where Bach lived for all his life, the established Lutheran church was torn between the majority, who were content with the somewhat ossified form of their church, and the new Pietist groups who had a nearly mystical approach to religion and hated all ceremony.

Pietists, as their name suggests, preferred a distinctly more devotional attitude to life and their faith than most Lutherans. They were not as strict as true Puritans and their religious practice was by no means dour. They tended to emphasize the contemplative and more spiritual aspects of protestantism, regarding much of the rest of life as mere distraction. Martin Luther (a religious reformer and founder of Lutheranism) stressed the importance of faith (as opposed to good deeds or mere outward appearances) in religion.

Pietists, however, fervently wished to extend this idea into a personal and rather emotive relationship between Christ and a believer. The relationship was brought about by the believer's individual acknowledgement of Christ, rather than by the intervention of pastors. Such an experience was described by the man acknowledged as the founder of Pietism, Philipp Jakcob Spencer (1635–1705), as a 'Christian awakening'. To the Pietists, therefore, music was a simple vehicle for fervent praise and rather sentimental devotion – and any elaboration of it was seen as a barrier to personal communication with God rather than an aid to it.

Lutherans, on the other hand, believed fundamentally in the God-given nature of talents, of creativity in all artistic forms, especially in music. Music itself could thus be a manifestation of praise, and the more excellent the composition, the greater the glory given to God.

Contemporary German church music

Musically, Germany in the 1680s was the meeting point of a number of influences. Form and formality in music were the main imports from France, while from Italy came a taste for panache and melody. Both were worked into the national preference for the baroque style and, in particular, the German love of counterpoint.

For more than 50 years prior to Bach's birth the major form in German music, both sacred and secular, had been the slow, formal 'hymn' called the *chorale*. Luther himself wrote many chorales that Bach was later to arrange and elaborate on. Chorales were also the basis for a variety of other forms. One of these variants was the *cantata*. It was defined as essentially a theatrical form by its first major proponent, Pastor Neumeister of Hamburg, in 1700, and as such the cantata was welcomed by the Lutherans who heard it – but the 'theatricality' was intolerable to the Pietists.

It was probably through such innovations as the

Eisenach (below), the town in which Bach was born in 1685 and where Martin Luther attended school. On the middle hill in the background is the Wartburg fortress where Luther took enforced refuge after the Diet of Worms, 1521 when he was placed under the ban of the empire by the Holy Roman Emperor, Charles V. While in the Wartburg Luther completed his translation of the Bible.

Archiv für Kunst und Geschichte

Philipp Jakob Spener (above) is acknowledged as the founder of Pietism, a spiritual movement for the revival of piety within the Lutheran doctrine in the 17th century. The Pietists were by no means dour in their devotion, but desired a more personal, direct contact with Christ, without the religious trappings which they saw creeping into Lutheran practices.

cantata that the musical differences between the two denominations, Lutheranism and Pietism, became more and more perceptible, until finally church music for the two became incompatible. Pietists wrote virulent tracts about the interference caused to meditation by 'bursts of laughter' from screeching Italian sopranos, the total distraction from personal prayer through the 'clashing din of instruments' that drowned both word and thought, and the 'seduction of the ear' by 'carnal' use of intellectual brilliance. They also preferred small prayer-meetings of enthusiasts to formal church services. The Lutherans went on simply developing and enlarging on the sounds and instruments which to them, in their well-established and well-attended church services, constituted an increasingly satisfactory means of worshipping their God.

The separation between these two protestant denominations was regrettable since many people, including Bach, shared sympathies with both the Pietist and orthodox Lutheran points of view. Bach, for instance, as much of his music in later life makes

Bach (left) saw his music as the expression of his deep religious feelings. From 1708–1718 he worked for the Duke of Saxe-Weimar as chamber musician and court organist. For the Duke's daily devotions, which took place in the castle church, known as the 'castle of heaven' (right) he produced some of his best organ music.

Archiv für Kunst und Geschichte

quite clear, wanted a warm, personal relationship with his God. He owned many books and tracts based on Pietist sentiments, including one by Spener. However, he and his family held orthodox Lutheran views and attended Lutheran services whenever possible.

Bach's early years

This then was the society, with its religion and musical background, into which Bach was born in Eisenach on 21 March 1685.

Eisenach itself was a great centre of Lutheranism. As a schoolboy Luther himself had stayed in the town at the home of the Cotta family (now called the Lutherhaus). In 1521, because of his reforming activities, Luther was placed under the ban of the empire by the Holy Roman Emperor, Charles V. For his own protection, and under the orders of the Elector of Saxony, he took enforced refuge at the Wartburg just south of Eisenach.

Bach's religion was founded on the views taken in from his family and on the formal religious education he received at school in Eisenach. After the deaths of both parents his musical education continued in the house of his eldest brother Johann Christoph, in Ohrdruf. Johann Christoph was organist at the church of Ohrdruf so it was not surprising that music and religion went hand in hand for Bach.

He attended school at Ohrdruf, studying the *Compendium locorum theologicorum,* a sort of religious instruction course written by the orthodox Lutheran theologian Leonhard Hutter of Wittenberg (and first published in 1610). From Ohrdruf Bach obtained a scholarship to a choir attached to the

Christian Richter 'Interior of the Himmelsburg Castle Chapel'. Kunstsammlungen zu Weimar

For the last 27 years of his life Bach lived and worked in Leipzig (right) where he was Kantor of the Thomasschule and civic music director. The first large-scale choral work which Bach wrote as Kantor was the St John Passion *(a page of which is shown below). It was first performed at vespers on Good Friday 1724 in the Nicolaikirche.*

Archiv für Kunst und Geschichte

Archiv für Kunst und Geschichte

Martinsschule in Lüneberg. Here he found himself surrounded by a tremendous wealth of church music past and contemporary at a formative time in his life.

It was probably at Lüneberg that he had his first taste of genuinely secular music. In his own music Bach never made a distinction between what he composed for the church and his compositions for his secular employers. For him, his music was always an expression of his own deep feelings. But here at Lüneberg he was entirely prepared to incorporate elements of influences from France and Italy into what he played and sang. Such 'foreign' innovations were intensely disliked by the Pietists, of course, and not even fully appreciated by the orthodox Lutherans at this time.

Bach's first church post was as organist and Kantor at Arnstadt. Part of his contract there stated that he was to 'take care of the organ, and to cultivate the fear of God, sobriety and a love of peace . . .' His actual duties were to play the organ for two hours on Sundays, at the Monday intercessions, and at matins on Thursdays; he was also responsible for a small choir at the Latin school.

It was not a happy time for him and for one reason or another his conduct came in for some strong criticism by his employers – the church committee.

From Arnstadt he moved to Mühlhausen where he secured the post of organist at St. Blasius's church. Within four months of taking up the appointment (in June 1707 at the age of 22), he married his first wife, Maria Barbara and settled down to the duties of playing the organ at all services. He was still determined, however, to introduce the new-style cantatas, modelled on Buxtehude's (for his own composing style had not yet matured). One of his first compositions here was *God is my King,* a cantata for the annual inauguration of the city council at the Mary's church. It was also at about this time that he wrote the motet (a form of chorale) *Actus Tragicus.*

Conflict at Mühlhausen

Unfortunately, he again ran into difficulties with his superiors. The pastor at St. Blasius, Johann Frohne, was a Pietist – and one with particularly strong views. It was at this time that Christian Wolff, a philosopher and protégé of Gottfried Liebniz, was becoming active at the town of Halle, a focus for progressive ideas in religion. His theories eventually led to his being given the title 'Prince of Enlightenment', and being hailed as the prophet of the age of enlightenment, then about to dawn. His questioning of establishment view led directly to the reinforcement and spread of Pietism – and Pastor Frohne and his congregation were quickly and unreservedly affected.

One of the parishioners of Mühlhausen, Georg Ahle, even published a treatise condemning the very style of music that Bach was attempting to introduce. And although Bach became renowned for his virtuoso organ playing (and his expert advice on organ reconstruction during visits to neighbouring cities), his doctrinal – and therefore musical – differences with his employer caused considerable tension. Furthermore, he was known to be on excellent terms with Pastor Frohne's much-disliked 'rival' in the city, the

DRAMA
PER MUSICA,
Welches
Bey dem Allerhöchsten
Crönungs-Feste
Des
Aller-Durchlauchtigsten und Groß-
mächtigsten
Augusti III.
Königs in Pohlen und Chur-
Fürsten zu Sachsen,
in unterthänigster Ehrfurcht aufgeführet wurde
in dem
COLLEGIO MUSICO
durch
J. S. B.
Leipzig, den Jan. 1734.
Gedruckt bey Bernhard Christoph Breitkopf.

music was considerable and Bach made special studies of the works of Vivaldi. But whereas such influences had previously inspired him to extravagance in writing and led to rebellion against church authority, now he was able to analyze more maturely what he heard, and even to try and improve upon it. Gradually, his music – just as his choice of themes had done – became less controversial, less ornamented and complex, though no less brilliant. As his style matured he omitted most of the exaggerated innovations on which he had insisted at Arnstadt and Mühlhausen.

From Weimar Bach went to Cöthen as Kapellmeister to Prince Leopold's secular court. While here, his wife Maria Barbara died. Her death came as a shattering blow. Suddenly he had four children to look after by himself. Plunged into grief, his renewed religious faith is expressed in his church music after 1720. It was also during his mourning that he buried himself in teaching the harpsichord to his sons and others. Eighteen months later, though, at the age of 36, he married Anna Magdalena, a singer in court and only seven years older than Bach's eldest daughter. This happy outcome of events after the death of his first wife increased Bach's gratitude to life in general as well as his reverence for God and the church in particular. His own private notebooks of the time are full of thoughts of love and death, and sentiments on scriptural themes.

The title page (far left) of one of a series of secular cantatas written by Bach for performance by the collegium musicum. He dedicated the cantatas to the new Elector of Saxony (below) who was crowned King of Poland on 19th February 1734. Bach probably hoped that he would be offered a position at court, but, in fact, only received a nominal title which involved writing occasional compositions.

orthodox Lutheran Archdeacon Georg Christian Eilmar of St Mary's, who became godfather to the Bach's first child in December 1708. By then, however, Bach had already resigned his post at Mühlhausen.

Organist at Weimar

He was lucky to find a vacancy as court organist to Wilhelm Ernst, Duke of Saxe-Weimar in Weimar. Duke Wilhelm was actually a fervent but rather dour Lutheran. The music he required at his daily devotions was strictly liturgical, and for these Bach wrote many of what are now his most famous cantatas. However, at the time, and perhaps conscious of his previous record, Bach was careful only to choose religious themes which were neither particularly Lutheran nor particularly Pietist.

In effect, Bach was in the process of devising his own personal religion, which was a combination of both Lutheranism and Pietism. Almost all the texts for his cantatas at that time were written by the orthodox Lutheran Salamo Franck – who shared Bach's liking for warm, personal expression of a relationship with God. Perhaps one of the most famous works by both Franck and Bach is the cantata *Komm, du süsse Todesstunde* ('Come, Thou Sweet Hour of Death').

In Weimar Bach began to put together what eventually became a surprisingly full and varied library of both Lutheran and Pietist books. However, although his personal religious commitment was taking firm shape, it was here he wrote cantatas which had a more secular starting point than those written for use in church. The well-known aria *Sheep May Safely Graze,* generally thought to refer to the Good Shepherd, is in fact part of a cantata extolling the Duke of Weimar's hunting prowess.

In music as well as in religion, then, Bach was aware of his own principles and standards and was able to use new influences in a more mature way. At the court, the influence of Italian and French styles of

The frontispiece (below) of the **Musicalisches Lexicon** *written by Johann Gottfried Walther, a second cousin of Bach's, illustrates the atmosphere of the church concerts for which Bach composed.*

The mature years

He left Cöthen in 1723 to become Kantor at St Thomas's in Leipzig. He was obliged to undergo a doctrinal examination in June 1722 and even before he got the job, to agree to some restrictive conditions imposed by the city councillors. The Kantor was the musical director for all five churches in the city; the population was generally Lutheran – but most of the clergy and also many of the Leipzig city councillors were Pietists.

At Leipzig, Bach settled down to write music for performance in the five churches under his direction. The first major work he produced during this period was the *St John Passion,* first performed in April 1724. During the next 20 years he is thought to have completed no fewer than 295 cantatas.

In this role it seemed that Bach could indulge his own enthusiasm for writing music in a fashion that related all the way back to the traditions of Luther himself. In particular, he could use the special combination of notes, chords or tempi according to the late medieval practices of 'musica theorica' and 'musica prattica': each musical figure was symbolic – one might represent the Trinity, another a specific aspect of Christ, and so on.

Even as he delighted in the musical theory of a bygone age – and was regarded as very old-fashioned for doing so – he was also refining his composition in a very contemporary way. His refinements, although suggesting a scenic background to the meaning of the words accompanying the music, resulted in a distinctly intellectual effect. This is evident in works like the *Christmas Oratorio* and the *Magnificat.*

In Leipzig, most of Bach's cantata texts were produced by the local Commissioner of the Post Office, Friedrich Henrici (who wrote under the name Picander). It was he who provided the text for the *St Matthew Passion,* first performed on Good Friday 1729. Although the work is thought of by many as the peak of Bach's church composition, the performance created a furore. Pietists in the congregation – all influential – hated it, finding it intolerably 'distracting'.

Bach enlarges his library

Whether a response to this reaction and criticism or not, at this time Bach greatly enlarged his collection of books on theology. He already possessed most of the works of Luther. In 1733 he purchased a version of Luther's Bible with a commentary, published in three volumes, by the theologian and mystic Abraham Calov of Wittenberg. His underlinings and marginal notes in the Bible make it clear that he gave it a very careful reading. Other spiritual publications Bach acquired at this time became the sources for later cantatas, though he occasionally changed the emphasis on these texts from strictly orthodox Lutheran to something between that and Pietism.

In the hope that he might obtain a position at court, Bach wrote two movements, the Kyrie and Gloria, of the *B Minor Mass* and presented them to the new Elector of Saxony, Friedrich August, who became King of Poland. Unfortunately, the only title he received was that of court composer.

Bach's life and work in Leipzig was often punctuated with disputes between himself and the church council. As before, these disputes usually arose because of differences between a strictly Lutheran and a Pietist approach to religious practice. Further Pietist condemnation came in 1737 from Johann Adolf Scheibe in Hamburg, who wrote scathingly about Bach's method of composition, although the controversy which followed ended with Scheibe being conciliatory and conceding that Bach was a skilled performer.

Whatever criticism he received in his time from those who did not share his religious views, Bach nevertheless continued to produce music which he saw as reflecting his own personal spiritual feelings.

Listener's guide

Any analysis of the life and times of a great composer cannot ignore his music, and this section examines in detail some of Bach's greatest and best-known works: the Brandenburg Concertos, the Toccata and Fugue in D minor, the Fantasia and Fugue in G minor, and Orchestral Suites 2 and 3. Along with sections on specific aspects of musical development of relevance to the works under discussion (for example, the development of counterpoint and the orchestral suite), the descriptions of the pieces of music can be read independently as an examination of Bach's musical achievements. However, for the fullest appreciation of this great composer's music, the programme notes are better read before going to a live performance or while listening to the recorded music. Suggestions for further listening are given within the text, and the Bibliography and the short descriptions of the lives and works of Bach's (and Haydn's) contemporaries on page 110 suggest other areas of study should you wish to learn more about their life, times and music.

Brandenburg Concertos nos. 2, 3 and 5

Bach composed the Brandenburg Concertos during a period he later described as idyllic. They have a brilliance of inventiveness that marks them as the ultimate flowering of the Baroque style.

The years Bach spent at Cöthen, from 1717 to 1723, came as a much-needed and creative respite from the religious environment in which he had been required to write and perform at Weimar. This period represents much of the 'middle' period of Bach's musical activity as a composer, when he was largely concerned with secular music, particularly with compositions for the orchestra and orchestral instruments. It was during this period that he wrote the Brandenburg Concertos.

It is not known precisely when the Concertos were written, only that they were completed by March 1721. Just eight months before, Bach's first wife Maria Barbara had died. However, he continued to compose and take part in the evening concerts at the court of Prince Leopold, where he was engaged as musical director. Prince Leopold was an enthusiastic musician and enjoyed playing the viola da gamba (the early equivalent of the cello), while Bach generally played the viola.

It was for these concerts that Bach wrote the Brandenburg Concertos; some of the viola da gamba parts are thought to have been written specifically to allow for the Prince's individual style of playing.

In mid-1721 Prince Leopold became engaged to a lady who had no musical interests, and was determined to persuade the Prince to give up such 'meaningless' pursuits with the 'servants'. Bach also intended to marry again and therefore was anxious to make his financial position secure. It was at this time that he wrote out a fair copy of the six Concertos, which he inscribed with a flattering and humble dedication to the Margrave Christian Ludwig of Brandenburg. The Concertos were then sent off to the Margrave's court in Berlin.

Christian Ludwig had invited Bach to submit some compositions when Bach had played for him in Berlin between June 1718 and March 1719. But if Bach had expected an immediate financial grant, or even an offer of employment, he was to be sadly disappointed. Nothing whatever came of his submission.

It had in any case been rather a hopeless gesture. The selection of instruments at the Margrave's court was smaller and quite different from that at Cöthen, and the concertos were therefore quite unsuitable for performance in Berlin. Yet it was because a copy was sent to the Margrave that the Concertos were preserved for posterity in their definitive form.

Programme notes

The true Baroque concerto was meant to be played 'concertedly', or 'in concert'. The three-movement form (a type of condensed suite) was initiated by the Italian Arcangelo Corelli (1653–1713). Known later as the concerto grosso, it featured the use of a large group of instruments – the *concerto* or *ripieno* – in contrast with a

Bach's six Brandenburg Concertos were composed for a chamber ensemble – a small orchestra of between seven and twelve players (left) – which included in its ranks many expert musicians.

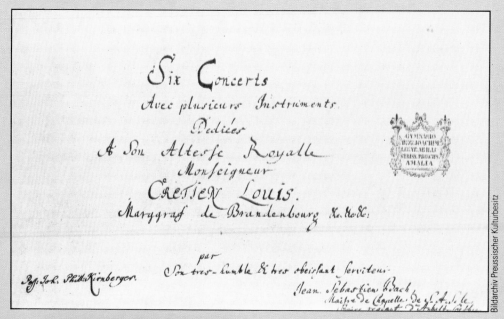

In March 1721 Bach dedicated the six Concertos to Ludwig, Margrave of Brandenburg (above). He made fair copies of the scores (title page – above right) and sent them to the Margrave's court at Berlin. However, he received no word of thanks and the Concertos were never used. Yet it is through the copies that the works were preserved.

Bach wrote the Brandenburg Concertos so that they could be performed in the concerts given by the orchestra at the court of Prince Leopold. The parts for the viola da gamba (right) were probably composed for the Prince himself, who played the instrument in the orchestra with great enthusiasm.

Concerto no. 2 in F major (BWV 1047)

This concerto is exceptional in many ways, but particularly because it contrasts four very different solo instruments – trumpet, recorder, oboe and violin – against a string orchestra of violins, viola and cello. The *basso continuo* – an accompaniment played from the bass-line – is performed by a harpsichord. As the solo instruments are so diverse the Concerto has a rare clarity; each instrument's melody-line can be heard individually within the counterpoint.

No. 2 is the only concerto to include a trumpet. The trumpet of Bach's day had no valves and therefore would have sounded less distinctive than the modern instrument. The part was written for Bach's friend Johann Schreiber, an expert trumpet player.

First movement: Allegro

Bach gave no direction concerning the speed at which this movement was to be performed, but it is generally played at a fair rate, with the consequence that a continuous running rhythm is set up from the beginning. Even as the main theme is introduced the cello, reinforced by the harpsichord, has started 'running', and from then on, almost to the end, at least one instrument is similarly dashing around in semiquavers.

After the introduction the solo violin proposes a second theme. With interjections from the string section, this theme is taken up one by one by the other soloists: oboe, recorder and finally trumpet. Although it is repeated, the soloists keep the theme to themselves – the string *ripieno* never touches it. The movement continues to use all three elements in various combinations of instruments and corresponding variations of mood and tone, finally coming to a momentary halt. This is followed by a

small group – the *concertino*. Each movement began with a question-and-answer 'dialogue' between the orchestral elements that led on to a general 'discussion'. It was this form that gradually evolved into the Baroque concerto, of which the six Brandenburg Concertos are an outstanding example.

The Brandenburg Concertos are all scored for a chamber ensemble – usually comprising between seven and twelve musicians. Although they follow the

classical Italian form, they have some very German traits: for example, the use of a trumpet in no. 2; the dominance of the harpsichord in no. 5; and the overall solid rhythmic basis of each one. To Bach, the most important element in his compositions was elaboration, by variation or any other device based on the individual theme. For this reason, his counterpoint is scintillating and brilliant, adding a final touch of genius to music that has been described as essentially introverted.

determined reiteration of the first theme by all the instruments in unison, which heralds the beginning of the end. The soloists play a final flourish as a quartet, and the movement comes to a triumphant conclusion.

Second movement: Andante

This movement is a marvellous combination of three elements and their variations: a consistently moving bass-line played by cello and harpsichord above which the soloists – flute, oboe and violin – alternate in playing the two short themes, sometimes described as 'sigh motifs'. As an example of counterpoint it can hardly be bettered. Look how the solo violin hands over the first theme to the oboe, which in turn passes it on the recorder.

Example 1

The violins and viola do not appear in the movement and the trumpet is the one soloist left out; the movement is predominately in the key of D minor – an almost impossible key for a valveless trumpet. Nevertheless the final flourish on the solo violin, which started the whole movement off, is a splendid trill that brings the key to D major.

Third movement: Allegro assai

In this bright clear fugue, all the instruments of the Concerto return. The trumpet begins, accompanied by the cello/harpsichord *continuo*. The theme is taken up by the oboe which begins on a lower note. An involved duet follows, broken by the entrance of the solo violin which repeats the theme in the original key. This is then taken up by the recorder and all four instruments strike up, allowing the cello and harpsichord a respite for a few bars. One-third of the way through the movement the strings of the orchestra (the *ripieno*) make an entrance, adding power

The tireless 'running' rhythm of the first movement of Concerto no. 2 – a sprightly Allegro – suggests a spirited hunting party enjoying the excitement of the chase (right).

Vittorio Amedeo Cignaroli 'Scovamento dei cervi'. Palazzina di Stupingi; Turin/Scala

Example 2

The final movement of Concerto no. 3 is a cheerful fugue, in which the main theme is started up on the violins and then lightheartedly imitated by the other instruments of the orchestra (Musical Example 2). The clarity and ingenuity of the ideas emphasizes the abstract nature of Bach's music, which, in its linear interweaving of melodic themes, finds a surprising counterpart in Mondrian's **Horizontal Tree** *design (above).*

violins, three violas and three cellos, with a double-bass and harpsichord *continuo*. Each set of instruments plays as a trio and has equal prominence within the whole composition.

This type of scoring represents the contemporary German love of *Spielmusik*: communal harmonizing using groups of similar or identical instruments. The Concerto is therefore as interesting to watch in performance as it is to hear.

First movement: Allegro moderato

As in no. 2, Bach did not write any notes about the speed of performance, but in this case the movement is ordinarily taken at a steady pace. The opening is forceful; each of the three trios plays in unison for maximum effect, and there are no individual parts until the rather long first theme has been completed by the violins.

and dimension to a momentary passage of emphasis. This occurs four times but is the *ripieno's* only role in the movement.

The soloists alternate and juggle the orginal theme until, in a mood of approaching climax in which the whole ensemble participates, the trumpet yet again repeats the theme with which it started the movement, this time as a concluding fanfare.

Concerto no. 3 in G major (BWV 1048)

It is generally thought that the Concertos nos. 3 and 6 were written before the others, certainly before 2 and 5. Although the music is no less brilliant it harks back to a style and form nearer to that of the earlier concerto grosso. Yet even here Bach was full of innovation: he scored no. 3 for three

Understanding music: what is counterpoint?

Counterpoint is almost as old as music itself. When the first monk broke away from the line of unison plain-chant to add a different melody, counterpoint – the placing of two or more musical lines against each other – was born. When speaking of counterpoint attention is usually drawn to the separate qualities of the two lines.

The rise of counterpoint theory

In Renaissance music counterpoint was the essence of musical discourse, rather like a conversation in which themes are presented and taken up by other voices. In a Mass setting by Palestrina (c.1525–94), for example, the basis of the composition is 'imitative'. This means that each part follows another in announcing, perhaps with some variations, a single melodic line and then combining it. During the Renaissance a whole theory of counterpoint arose, but just at the same time as this theory emerged music moved forward.

The dawning age of the Baroque in

Counterpoint is a combination of simultaneous 'voices', each of significance in itself, with the whole resulting in a rich texture, like the patterns of light on the floor of this Dutch interior (below).

E. de Witte 'Woman playing the Harpsichord' (detail). Museum Boymans van Beuningen/State-Owned Art Collections Department, The Hague

early 17th-century Italy swept conventional counterpoint aside and instead asserted the primacy of the single vocal or instrumental monody (song for one voice), accompanied by a *basso continuo* (a bass part with harmonies placed above it). But the centuries-old art of counterpoint continued to be revered, and was still taught even at a time when it was not widely practised except in deliberately old-fashioned sacred compositions.

As Baroque music developed in complexity, counterpoint re-emerged as a strong force and eventually reasserted itself as a fundamental element in composition. Far from having inhibited counterpoint, the combination of voices over a *basso continuo* stimulated a type of composition in which two upper voices (violins, for example) had imitative parts over a bass line, which also joined in the counterpoint of the theme. The trio sonata (as these three-line works were called) soon became a staple diet of the later Baroque: Corelli, Vivaldi, Handel and other composers wrote many examples.

The art of the fugue

As contrapuntal composition was elaborated the fugue – the most familiar fixed form of counterpoint – also became established. Many books have been written about how to compose strict fugues, but the greatest composers rarely followed these rather narrow and confined plans. Nevertheless, a few 'signposts' regularly occur in the course of a fugue.

The exposition of a fugue consists of each voice presenting the theme, or subject, of the work. One voice announces the theme, then a second voice presents it at a different pitch and this is called the 'answer'. Meanwhile, the first voice will continue with what is generally called the 'countersubject'. This is usually designed to contrast with the original fugue theme. Then, as the second voice takes up and continues with the countersubject, the third voice enters, and the first voice continues freely; and so on until the exposition of the fugue is complete.

After this exposition there may be 'episodes' using new material, or material derived from the subject, answer or countersubject. These episodes are interspersed with more regular sections in which the fugue's subject again enters formally – but there is not necessarily another complete run through of it in all parts. Various other devices can also be used to diversify this process. The term

The British Library

The art of counterpoint developed from the 9th century onwards and probably had its origins in monastic singing traditions (above).

'stretto' is used when the entries of the fugue subject are compressed and overlap; 'augmentation' is used when the fugue subject is halved in speed, and so appears in long notes among the quicker motion of the other parts; and 'diminution' refers to the reverse procedure, by which the fugue subject appears with the speed doubled.

Bach and counterpoint

An understanding of these techniques is not necessary in order to appreciate the greatest monuments of contrapuntal art from the period of the late Baroque. For J. S. Bach in particular, counterpoint lay at the very root of his art. The 48 Preludes and Fugues, which appeared in two books, explore an infinitely wide range of fugal devices. Bach's *Goldberg Variations* explore another very particular contrapuntal device, that of canon, in which the fugue-like imitation between the parts is always exact, as it is if you sing the round Frère Jacques. And in *The Art of Fugue,* one of the greatest works of Bach's last decade, he brought the art of Baroque counterpoint to its climax in a dazzling display of the variety that could be extracted from a single musical theme. Counterpoint continues to be a fundamental element in musical composition, but few would dispute that in the music of J. S. Bach its highest potential was realized.

From then on each trio battles for the main theme, using the secondary theme introduced at the beginning by the violas as well as recognizable derivations of both. Fifty years after Bach composed the Concerto, this became known as 'development' and was a feature of post-Baroque Classical music. But the real development is to come, as approximately one third of the way through this exceptionally long movement there is a shift of emphasis. Led by the violins, the instruments begin a restive exploration in which combinations of the first three notes of the initial theme are contrasted with the theme itself in various guises. For a moment there is a brief return to the familiar, then the 'search' is taken up again with an increasing sense of desperation. After each instrument has searched exhaustively a short unison sequence heralds the familiar 'home' tune in the 'home' key. The theme is repeated joyfully and triumphantly and the movement ends.

Second movement: Adagio
As written, Bach's second movement consisted solely of two chords (A minor and B major) technically called a Phrygian cadence. This was a recognized device used in two different circumstances. First, if the movement was very long an ultra-short second movement balanced the programme while observing the obligatory three-movement form. Second, it was sometimes used as an indication that at this point improvisation was not only acceptable but expected, as long as the two chords written were played to begin or end.

In the 20th century the latter alternative has generally been favoured. Although the first movement of no. 3 is long, it is not interminable. It is thought that Bach may well have preferred to improvise music himself, presumably at the keyboard and unaccompanied, and that the orchestra would have come in for the final cadence.

In some preformances, the Largo (third) movement of Bach's Sonata in G (BWV 1021) is inserted. It is both tuneful and slightly mournful, providing an appropriate bridge between the good-humoured and sprightly first movement and the almost abandoned gaiety of the third.

The movement ends with the full orchestral cadence.

Third movement: Allegro
The last movement is a fugue. It is characterized by simplicity, not only in the writing but by the fact that it is in two distinctive parts. The first section is twelve bars long and is repeated before the second, 36-bar section which is also repeated.

The trio of cellos plays in unison throughout the movement. Even the violas begin the fugue in this way although for the purpose of harmony the violas start before their turn. There is a carefree mood, and the theme begun by the violins is tossed about rather recklessly; within three bars the first violin has turned the theme upside down.

The remainder of the movement is no less fast and furious, despite the second section starting in a minor key. The whole movement is infused with elegant delicacy and a genuine spirit of fun. There are some graceful and difficult flourishes from the first violin and first viola, and the movement concludes with a false but delightful 'raggedness'.

Bach styled the second movement of the Fifth Concerto as a galant, *a stately dance then highly fashionable at the French and German courts. The term was very popular in the 18th century: 'Being* galant' *was, in Voltaire's words, 'to seek to please', while the* galant *style of painting (right) was characterized by its lightness, grace and elegance.*

The first page of the Brandenburg Concerto no. 5, in Bach's neat hand (below). Several solo instruments feature in this Concerto and these are listed across the top of the page. However, as the leading role is played by the keyboard instrument it sounds almost like a harpsichord concerto.

Jean-Baptiste Pater/Fête Champêtre/Chris Barker/Victoria and Albert Museum

Concerto no. 5 in D major (BWV 1050)

Bach's original title for this Concerto cites three solo instruments – harpsichord, violin and flute – which play in contrast with a string trio and double-bass *continuo*. However from the first movement it is evident that the harpsichord is utterly dominant. No fewer than 65 bars are allotted to it and for this reason the Concerto is sometimes referred to as the first harpsichord concerto. The monopoly of the harpsichord is not carried over to the other movements to the same extent, but by then the overall feeling of the work has been established. Bach undoubtedly would have played the harpsichord for this Concerto, rather than his preferred viola.

First movement: Allegro

The flute is the only instrument that does not start off with the rest, as the violins, both solo and *ripieno,* take up the initial theme. Once this has been played the soloists stand out, and apart from interjections by the orchestra following the pattern of the original theme, all three solo instruments take over the proceedings.

In the score Bach differentiates carefully between the harpsichord as an accompanying instrument and as a solo one. The music for the solo part is fully written out for both hands. However, when the instrument is accompanying as part of the *continuo* with the double-bass, there is only an indication for the left hand, with numbers beneath to suggest the right hand's part – a system known as 'figured bass'.

From the first, the harpsichord begins to exhibit extra virtuosity. Some awe-inspiring runs are called for, while other instruments are doing much less above. Although the entire ensemble comes in for a time with the harpsichord, the keyboard instrument eventually takes over. When the solo ends the rest of the ensemble (except for the flute) reiterates the initial theme and brings the movement to an end.

Second movement: Affettuoso

This movement is a *galant:* a stately and elegant piece in the Franco-German court fashion then coming into vogue, and is an attempt by Bach to be thoroughly up to date. Only the three soloists take part – the *ripieno* makes no appearance – and the harpsichord is the only instrument that is not given a rest during the movement. This is because it is acting as a soloist for two-thirds of the piece, and as an accompaniment for the remainder.

Third movement: Allegro

Like the *galant,* this too is a dance: a lively *gigue* or jig in 2/4 time. Such pieces were usually planned to end in a suite of dances.

This *gigue* is also an extended fugue. The solo violin begins and is soon joined by the flute, followed independently first by the harpsichordist's left hand and then

Jan Vermeer 'The Artist in his Studio'. Kunsthistorisches Museum, Vienna/Bridgeman Art Library

by the right. All four instruments play a lively and lilting theme which the rest of the ensemble are allowed a 'scent' of eventually. The harpsichord inevitably begins to make its presence felt, but with less success than might have been expected. The flute and solo violin combine to keep the harpsichord from having it all its own way. And despite a short solo by the keyboard instrument the whole lilting dance sways on through the other instruments, even obliging the harpsichord to take a complete rest for seven bars while the other soloists repeat the initial theme. This 'indignity' is avenged when once again the fugal form reasserts itself and the harpsichord enters. All the other instruments join in and after a rousing restatement of the theme the dance and the Concerto finally come to an end.

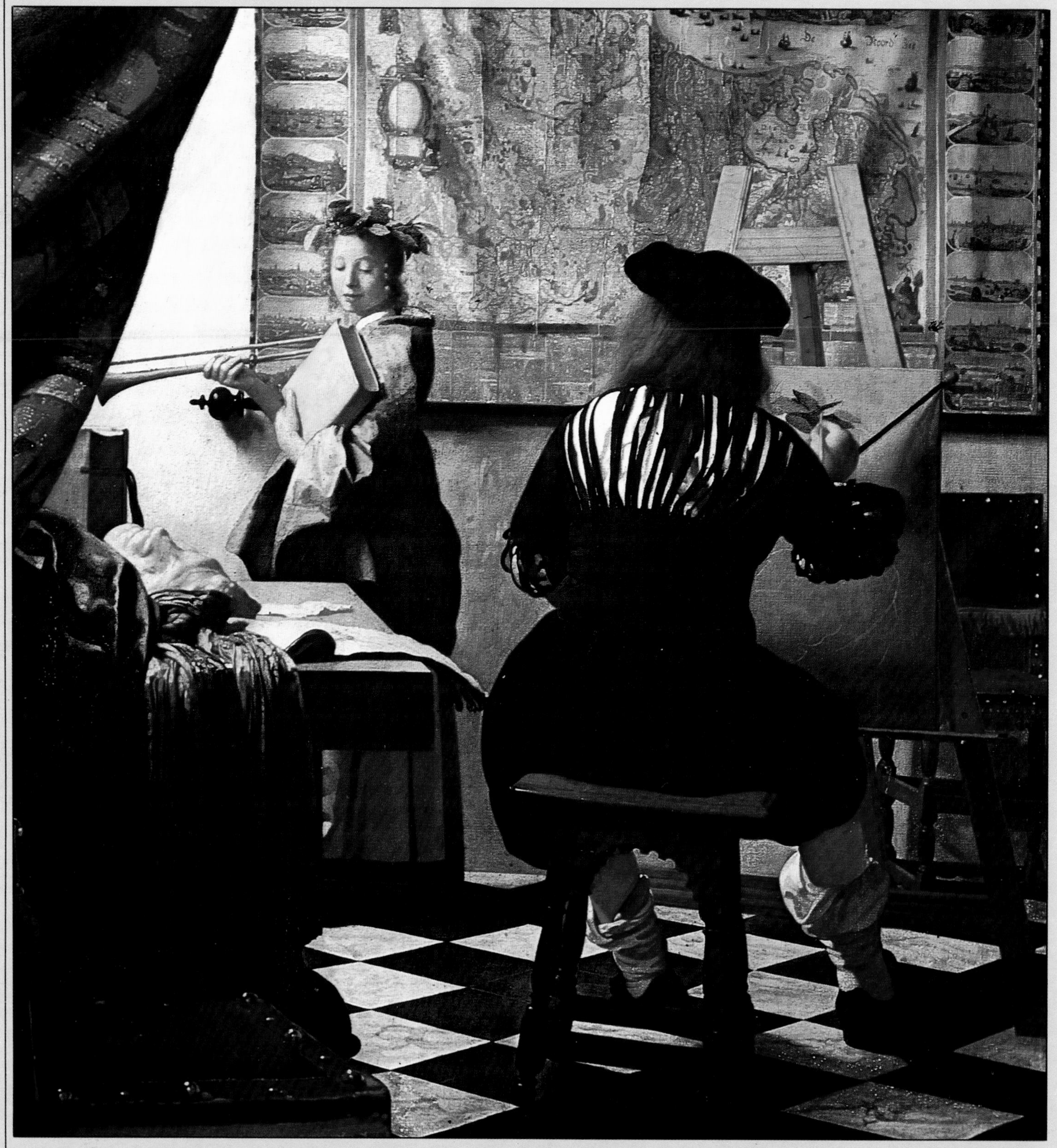

Many of Bach's preoccupations in the Brandenburg Concertos seem to be shared by the Dutch painter Vermeer (his* Allegory of Painting *is shown above). The works of both painter and composer are characterized by a brilliant handling of colour, a fascination with contrasting textures, an interest in spatial relationships, and a pervasive mood of intimacy and introspection.

Great interpreters

Mike Evans

The distinguished conductor and harpsichordist Raymond Leppard (above) has made many fine recordings with the ECO (above right).

Mike Goddard/English Chamber Orchestra

Raymond Leppard (conductor and harpsichordist)
Leppard, born in England in 1927, studied at Trinity College, Cambridge, from 1948 to 1952. He made his London début in 1952 at Wigmore hall, and in the same year formed the Leppard Ensemble in London. He also quickly established himself as a harpsichordist, playing with Yehudi Menuhin among others. He returned to Trinity College in 1958 as a lecturer in music and a Fellow, staying there for three years. Concurrently, he pursued his conducting career and formed his own orchestra, which later merged with the Goldsmith Orchestra.

In 1962 he prepared a performing edition of Monteverdi's *Coronation of Poppaea* for Glyndebourne, and delivered it to a new and appreciative audience. This led to a series of revivals of long-neglected operas by both Monteverdi and Cavalli which brought Leppard much recognition.

His work with the ECO has centred mainly on composers from the 17th and 18th centuries. He has recorded all the orchestral music of Handel, apart from the Organ Concertos, as well as Monteverdi's complete Madrigals of Love and War series. From 1973 to 1980 he was principal conductor of the BBC Northern Orchestra, and in this post he extended his repertoire greatly.

His conducting is distinguished by a great sense of colour and dynamism, along with crispness of orchestral articulation. He concentrates on bringing out the essential character of the works he performs while avoiding the sometimes dry and unrewarding approach adopted in many more authentic performances and interpretations in the early music field.

Today he is looked on as a figure of great authority, both for his work as a player and for his detailed knowledge of the pre-romantic repertoire.

The English Chamber Orchestra
The ECO was formed in 1948 under the title of the Goldsbrough Orchestra. In its first decade as a performing unit it concentrated on the 18th-century repertoire, often appearing in radio broadcasts and, more infrequently, on the public stage.

The name of the group was changed in 1960 to the ECO and, as such, it quickly broadened its musical horizons. In particular, it formed a close association with the English Opera Group and the Aldeburgh Festival. This naturally led to strong ties with Benjamin Britten and a leading part in the first performances of many of his operatic and concert works.

The ECO has been an independent and self-governing orchestra since it began. It has been well represented on records across a vast field, and with a variety of distinguished conductors and soloists. The ECO during some of their most distinguished recordings were as follows:

Violins:	José Luis Garcia, Simon Standage, Adrian Levine
Violas:	Quintin Ballardie, Rüsen Gunes, Andrew Williams
Cellos:	Olga Hegedus, Stephen Orton, Anita Lasker
Doublebass:	Rodney Slatford
Oboe:	Neil Black
Recorder:	David Munrow
Flute:	Richard Adeney
Trumpet:	John Williams
Harpsichord and conductor:	Raymond Leppard

FURTHER LISTENING

Bach orchestral and vocal works
Violin Concerto in A Minor, BWV 1041
Bach wrote most of his concertos during his stay at Cöthen between 1717 and 1723. In this period he was brought into contact with much of the latest in musical composition, and wrote a collection of violin concertos in the style of Vivaldi. Few of them survive in their original form, the A Minor being one of only three. But the beauty and grace of the solo instrument's lines interweaving with the ensemble reveal Bach's mastery of the Italian form. The music is cogently written and deeply expressive.

Double Violin Concerto in D Minor, BWV 1043
This Concerto was written in 1720 and remains to this day Bach's most popular in this form: justifiably, as it is the most beautiful. Adhering to the standard three-movement concerto structure, the work moves through a lively *Vivace,* where the principal two themes are stated and brilliantly developed. The *Largo* which follows is radiantly beautiful and reaches profound depths of expression. The final movement brings the work to a balanced and satisfying conclusion.

St Matthew Passion
Bach wrote five complete Passions, though only two have come down to us in their entirety; the *St Matthew* and *St John*. His religious compositions are amongst his most overwhelming achievements, and the Passions are one of the jewels of our cultural heritage. The *St Matthew* is a gigantic work, both in terms of length and in the forces called for. But the end result fully justifies the expanded means of expression.

LISTENER'S GUIDE
Organ works

Bach's organ pieces, like the splendid instruments for which they were written, were crafted for the glory of God. Works of consummate artistry, they have proved a lasting source of inspiration.

The Baroque era was a time of extreme religious, social and artistic contrasts – contrasts which found musical expression in the dramatic and colourful operas and concertos and the elaborate church music of Italy, the splendour of works composed for the French courts, and the more devotional and abstract music of Germany. Naturally, the style of one country affected another's: Heinrich Schütz, born 100 years before Bach, studied with Giovanni Gabrieli and brought back to Protestant Germany many elements of the ornate style of Catholic Venice. And the influence and might of Louis XIV's sumptuous court at Versailles reached its zenith when Bach was a boy. It was the envy of the rulers of the smaller German principalities, who aspired to the same opulence and brilliance.

Geographically, Germany was well placed to absorb both French and Italian influences, but while France and Italy were Catholic, North Germany had adopted the reformed faith of Martin Luther. North German church music in Bach's time was built on congregational participation and chorale tunes, some adapted from folk melodies and popular songs, others written by Luther himself or by other German composers. Many of these strong melodies are still in use in churches today. French and Italian influences served to expand and elaborate this basic musical style – and it is in Bach's music that we can hear a near-perfect synthesis of styles.

The religious background

Bach was born 37 years after the end of the Thirty Years' War in 1648. This bitter, straggling conflict inflamed differences between catholic and protestant and quickly turned to the more political issues of acquiring and protecting territory. It involved almost all Europe and crippled Germany, which was at the centre of hostilities. What remained of the German population – some historians estimate that nearly half perished – huddled together in the free cities and hundreds of small states. It was to be over 200 years before they achieved national unity. Small wonder, in the midst of all this chaos, that German artists looked to countries with a strong sense of artistic identity like France and Italy for ideas and inspiration. Nor was it surprising that the stronger German towns, cities and courts took their dearly-bought religious and political independence so seriously.

The church became one of the major focal points in the town and church music became increasingly important. Certainly the growing fashion for opera in the rest of Europe resulted in the building of opera houses in large cities such as Hamburg, but in Germany opera was still overshadowed by church and instrumental music. So the position of director of music, or Kantor, at a major city church was important and highly sought-after. With it came responsibility for the town's many music

Pieter Saenredam 'The Grote Kerk, Haarlem' The National Gallery, London

Bach's organ music draws on the two major and contrasting styles of the Baroque era: the ornate and colourful Franco-Italian tradition (reflected in this elaborate costume design for an early opera intermezzo – left) and the more devotional, abstract tradition of the North, echoed in the geometric lines of Saenredam's cool church interior (right).

Riblinteca Nazionale, Florence/Scale

clubs and lecturing posts at the local university. To be Kapellmeister, or in charge of music at one of the courts, was equally prestigious. Indeed, to list the musicians who were privileged to hold these posts is to give the roll of honour in 17th-century German music: Schütz, Pachelbel, Buxtehude and Telemann; all held church or court posts and, inevitably, their appointments affected the music they wrote.

This is the background to Bach's music. Certainly his own church posts had a profound effect upon his compositions for the organ – he was, above all, a practical and practising musician. His first three jobs

as a young man were organist's posts at Arnstadt (1703), Mühlhausen (1707) and Weimar (1708–17), and this is the period which saw the production of most of his organ music.

Although Bach's fame as an organist was widespread, by the time of his death his artistic position was isolated. He had taken his layered, many-voiced fugal style to the peak of perfection and it was soon to be superceded by a simpler, more melodic form. The new music, of which Bach's own son Carl Philipp Emanuel was a pioneer, was far less centred on the church and increasingly involved the piano – the new instrument which was to change the whole

aspect of domestic music-making.

When Bach died in 1750, his music died with him – little of it had been published and many manuscripts were irretrievably lost. It was well into the 19th century before interest was revived: Mendelssohn's performance in 1829 of the *St Matthew Passion* was a landmark, and the Romantic composers Schumann, Chopin, Liszt and Wagner all saw the importance and magnitude of his music.

Organ building
Bach's lifetime saw the golden age of organ building. In the non-opera biased countries of northern Europe it reached a level of

mechanical ingenuity and excellence that for many can be equalled today only by imitation. Arp Schnitger (1648–1720) and Gottfried Silbermann (1683–1753) were masters of organ design, voicing and construction; their achievements rank no lower than those of Stradivari or Guarneri with the violin.

Although most of the organs that Bach played were relatively modest, other instruments were very large – with four *manuals* or keyboards, a pedal board (to be played with the feet) and around 70 speaking stops. The organs of St Nicholas's Church, Hamburg and the Johanniskirche in Lüneberg, for example, were famous throughout Europe. The most important part of the typical Baroque organ was the *Prinzipal* or diapason section, which provided the body tone of the instrument. Next in importance were the quieter flue pipes, with a smaller number of 'string' or 'reed' stops imitating the sound of orchestral instruments. These were used for added colour and contrast and for solo passages. Very important were the mixture stops – three or five ranks of pipes tuned to the harmonics of the fundamental sound – which gave brilliance and bite to the overall sound and helped to project it in a large building. Real pitch was based on 8-foot pipes; 16-foot and 32-foot pipes produced sound an octave and two octaves lower, 4-foot and 2-foot pipes an octave and two octaves higher.

On a large instrument the main stops would be grouped on the *Hauptwerk* (main organ); other stops would be grouped on the *Brustwerk* (breast organ, below the main organ) and on the *Oberwerk* (upper organ, with the pipes placed near the top of the instrument). At the organist's back was the *Rückpositiv* (literally the 'back organ', but often called the chair or choir organ). Ideally, each section would have its own manual, although four-manual instruments were rare. The baroque organ did not have the weight and volume of sound that we associate with 19th- and 20th-century

instruments; more important was the quality of tone and the skill and imagination of registration (the availability of different sound 'colours' with which to interpret the music).

We can judge Bach's fame as an organist today by the compositions he has left – works which form the core of the instrument's repertoire. During his lifetime, however, he was equally famous as an expert in organ building and design, and he travelled widely testing out new instruments. His son Carl Philipp Emanual wrote:

'He understood the whole building of organs to the highest degree ... Organists were terrified when he sat down to play on their instruments and drew the stops in his own manner, for they thought that the effect would not be as good as he was planning it; but they heard an effect which astounded them. The first thing he would do in trying an organ was this. He would say in jest, "Above all, I must know whether the organ has good lungs", and, to find out, he would draw out every speaking stop, and play in the fullest and richest texture. At this the organ-builder would often grow quite pale with fright.'

Programme notes

The Weimar court was where Bach composed most of his organ music, and

In this engraving from Praetorius's Theatrum instrumentorum (1620), one of three volumes on musical practice and theory, two men use their body-weight to work the bellows of a large organ so as to pump enough air into the pipes (right). Praetorius's treatise, with its particularly thorough section on the organ, testifies to the prominent position of the instrument at the beginning of the Baroque period.

AISA

This panel from Van Eyck's altarpiece at Ghent (1432), depicting angel musicians (right), illustrates the role the organ has historically played in the glorification of God. The highly decorated organs of the Baroque period – an example is shown on the far right – were designed to have much the same impact as an altarpiece – serving as a visible as well as an audible hymn of praise. Indeed, as much work was devoted to these great architectural edifices, topped with angels and heraldic coats of arms, as went into the decoration of the high altar itself. Bach would have played on such an instrument and, as an expert in organ building and design, would have appreciated the exquisite craftsmanship.

where he also established beyond a doubt his supremacy as a virtuoso. Many of the works of this period were not based on chorale melodies but grew from wholly original material.

Toccata and Fugue in D minor (BWV 565)

This youthful work was probably written around the time of Bach's famous visit to Lünebeck to hear Buxtehude – around 1705, before his appointment to Weimar. It is probably his best-known work, so it is ironic that doubts have been cast on whether or not Bach actually wrote it. Its rhapsodic, improvisatory style is so unusual that it has been suggested that it is an early transcription of an unknown work for violin, since many of its effects are suited to a stringed instrument.

The term *Toccata* (from the Italian *toccare:* to touch) has come to mean a display piece, usually for keyboard. This Toccata is essentially just that and the dramatic opening bars must be the most famous in all organ music. The form is very simple: the prelude (that is, the toccata) is followed by a fugue, rounded off by a cadenza-like postlude. The short toccata is based on three sections: the opening, immediately followed by rapid triplets pushing the music along faster, and then an urgent tag of melody over a repeated-note figure – all of it designed to show off

different aspects of keyboard effects. Except at the end, the pedals have very little to do in the toccata, which closes with a return to the triplets near the opening and massive block chords over a short, but imposing, pedal solo.

Example 1

This fugue is not one of Bach's tightest, and again the pedals have a relatively easy time. Most of the interest is in the keyboard figuration – the first pedal entry heralds even more elaborate keyboard work, and the postlude is almost operatic in its dramatic changes of tempo from very slow to very fast, punctuated by flashes of swirling scales.

Whatever the interpretations put on this work – from Walt Disney's use of it in his film *Fantasia* to one commentator's view of it as 'storm' music – its impact as a display piece is never in doubt.

Fantasia and Fugue in G minor (BWV 542)

The date of this piece is not certain – nor is it sure whether the two movements belong together. The Fantasia was probably composed at Weimar after 1712; the fugue probably dates from earlier. Both were

The imposing organ at St Johannis, Zittau (right) was built by Gottfried Silbermann – now recognized as one of the greatest organ builders of all time. Silbermann was organ builder to the court of Saxony and an acquaintance of Bach and his pupil Ludwig Krebs.

Michael Gillingham

Understanding music: church music

Praising God in music is an established element of worship in many religious traditions. The early Christians readily adopted the practice from Judaism where music played a dominant part. As Christianity spread across Europe, Jewish influences were matched by those from Greece and Rome and a considerable body of Latin chants was built up, which varied from region to region. By the end of the sixth century, Pope Gregory the Great had established a collection of over 3,000 chants which became the musical foundation of the Roman liturgy and Gregorian chant, or plainchant, which is still used today.

It was at Notre Dame in Paris that composers first began to exploit the possibilities of combining several voices together, and it is to Guillaume de Machaut (c. 1300–1377) that we owe the first complete polyphonic setting of the mass. His *Messe de Nôtre Dame* is a striking example of the medieval style. By the 16th century, the polyphonic style had been refined and developed into an elaborate and expressive musical language, capable of conveying intense emotion, as epitomized in the music of Josquin des Prés (c. 1440–1521). But its continued development was disrupted as the Reformation spread across Europe.

In England the traditional Latin verses were replaced by their English equivalents. During Cromwell's Commonwealth, music was banned from churches altogether, although the restoration of Charles II soon made up for past deficiencies with the establishment in the Chapel Royal of a string orchestra to accompany the singers and the services of some of England's finest composers, including Purcell.

In Italy, following the Council of Trent in 1545, composers were urged to return to simpler means of expression, as exemplified in the serene Masses of Palestrina, although a few years later, St Mark's in Venice gave birth to a new tradition of music of overwhelming spatial effect.

In Germany, the southern states, remaining predominantly Catholic, continued to follow the stylistic lead of Italy, while in the north, the Lutheran Church established its own tradition, based on the singing of simple chorales – similar to English hymn tunes.

It was in the employ of the Lutheran Church that J. S. Bach spent most of his life, and made possibly the greatest single contribution of any composer to church music – composing a wealth of material which is still the focal point of the Lutheran tradition.

Bach's great contribution marked the end of an era. But, as with so many composers, Bach can be seen to be looking forward as well as back. Among this large-scale church works was his elaborate and lengthy Mass in B minor; this, in effect, became the first of a new genre of works which, in the course of the 19th century, transported the liturgy away from the church and into the concert hall. The Masses of Haydn and Mozart, although still designed for liturgical use in the lavish musical establishments of their noble patrons, owe much of their style to the symphonies and operas of their creators. With Beethoven's *Missa Solemnis,* this symphonic approach reaches epic proportions and enters the realm of the 19th-century concert mass. In keeping with the Romantic ideals of the age, many composers expressed their religious fervour through large-scale settings of the mass and other liturgical texts, among them, Berlioz who prescribed eight pairs of timpani for his Requiem *(Grande Messe des Morts)* and a choir of 600 children's voices for the Te Deum; while Rossini's Stabat Mater and Verdi's Requiem provided quite profane delights in their operatic lyricism.

In the 20th century, sacred works for the concert hall continue to abound: the Masses of Kodaly, Stravinsky, Poulenc and Vaughan Williams are all works of haunting beauty, while the organ repertoire has been greatly enriched by the many and varied compositions of Messiaen.

While the well-known, 19th-century composers wrote sacred music of symphonic proportions, rural piety found simple, but no less fervent expression in choral singing (below).

Thomas Webster 'The Village Choir' Victoria and Albert Museum

revised some years later when Bach was in Cöthen. The fugue subject is similar to a Dutch folksong – probably intended as a compliment to the 97-year-old Dutch organist Johann Adam Reincken (1623–1722) for whom Bach played during this visit.

The elaborate Fantasia falls into five clearly defined sections. The opening is almost like a cadenza, the swirling figuration punctuated by huge chords and anchored to a pedal bass. This yields to a contrasting statement in four parts, with a moving pedal line and with much imitation between the voices. The main material

Bach's Fantasia and Fugue in G minor is made up of two movements, which may have been written as separate pieces. The Fugue is reminiscent of a Dutch folksong in a light-hearted vein (left), and was probably composed as a tribute to the aged Dutch organist Johann Adam Reincken.

returns, this time with more elaborate harmony and leading to a repeat of the contrapuntal material. A memorable passage of rising chords over a gently falling pedal line eventually opens out into the final returns of the opening.

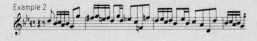

Example 2

This fugue is one of the most completely tuneful that Bach ever wrote and its various entries are immediately recognizable. The fugue is central to the instrumental music of the Baroque era. The form varies enormously, but all fugues start with the exposition, where each voice enters separately with the subject, building up a complex web of sound. This is usually relieved by the simpler texture of an episode, the function of which is to move to another key for a repeat of the fugue. A further episode may revert to the home key and the fugue's conclusion.

Prelude and Fugue in E minor (BWV 548)

This work was written between 1725 and 1728, when Bach was working as Kantor to St Thomas's Church in Leipzig. Its huge scale and detailed organization have led one Bach scholar to call it 'an organ symphony in two movements'. It is certainly among the most important works of Bach's late period.

The prelude is like a concerto in the way it uses blocks of highly characterized material in an elaborate musical mosaic. The opening *ritornello* (a short passage that is repeated throughout a movement) is easily identified by the massive octave leaps in the pedal, and its statuesque proportions bind the prelude together. Another important episode that occurs three times is a lightly scored passage,

The same fertility of invention which characterizes Bach's organ compositions is displayed in this mosaic, lining the dome of St Clemente's church in Rome (right). Illustrating the 'Tree of Life', it could almost be a visual description of the way in which Bach's organ music builds and unfolds, branching out into endlessly creative variations. And, as with the music, glittering fragments combine to create a magnificent whole.

without pedals, with a lilting rhythm that provides relief from the thickly-textured music of the rest of the prelude.

Example 3

The fugue is nicknamed 'The Wedge' because of the way in which the subject gradually opens out in wider and wider intervals. Its form is unusual in that the opening section is repeated almost note for note at the end. The middle section is like a sonata development and is almost exactly twice as long as the main fugue; the fugal texture is abandoned in favour of more fluid material based on rushing scales and other keyboard effects, with interjections of the opening of the fugue subject both on pedals and manuals which prepare the listener for the repeat of the fugue.

Passacaglia and Fugue in C minor (BWV 582)
Like the Toccata and Fugue in D minor, this is an early work and was probably composed before Bach moved to Weimar. The Passacaglia (or Chaconne, as it was also known) was originally a slow dance with three beats to the bar but, by the 18th century, it had come to mean a set of variations built over a repeated ground bass. Bach's magnificent example is based on a simple eight-bar theme.

Example 4

The first four bars of this had been used by the French composer André Raison in one of his organ works.

After the solo statement of the Passacaglia theme, Bach builds a sequence of 20 variations that grow in complexity. They are organized into two sets of ten variations and the first climax comes at the end of variation 10, when for the first time the pedal part itself has a variant of the theme. Variation 11 is without pedals and places the theme in the highest register where it stays for the quickly gathering complexity of variation 12. The next three, for manuals only, thin out the texture to its bare essentials, leaving the last five to build up the tension again in a magnificent climax that leads straight into the fugue. This is a double fugue that takes the first half of the Passacaglia theme and combines it with a countersubject, both of which run throughout.

The endless fertility of imagination with which the variations evolve and the skilful gathering and subsiding climaxes make this work one of Bach's greatest masterpieces.

Great interpreters

Karl Richter

Richter was a Bach specialist, and spent the greater portion of his professional life developing and refining his understanding of the composer's works.

Born in Plauen, Saxony, the son of a clergyman, Richter from the very first was involved in church tradition and the music of Bach. He sang as a boy in the Dresden Kreuzchor, then moved on to Leipzig where he studied with such figures as Rudolf Mauersberger and Karl Straube. He remained in Leipzig for the rest of the 1940s, becoming Choirmaster of Leipzig's Christ Church in 1946 and organist at St Thomas's Church in 1947. From this point on he pursued his career at several levels simultaneously; as a conductor, organist and harpsichordist.

In 1951 he took up the position of Kantor at Munich's St Mark's Church. This role involved him in every facet of the church's musical life. By this time his authority as an exponent of Bach was already being recognized. In the same year he joined the teaching staff at Munich's Hochschule für Musik. By 1956, after a record of success, he was appointed Professor at the same school.

From this time on, Richter was increasingly active as an organizer, conductor and player of the music of Bach: he was the Choirmaster of the Munich Bach Choir, conductor and founder of the Munich Bach Orchestra, and frequent keyboardist at Bach recitals, both inside and outside church. From 1952 onwards, Richter and his ensembles were involved in making records and, in association with DG Archiv Produktion, recorded an astonishing amount of the old master's music, from the Passions through to the Brandenburg

Concertos and the keyboard works. Many of these records have won high praise.

Richter is regarded today as a leading authority on Bach's music. His interpretative style lies in between romanticism and the newer movement back to complete historical authenticity. It is a literal one with marked and deliberate rhythmic accents, and although he has been labelled a stiff player of the organ at times, especially in the more speedy passages, his performances of Bach and Handel have an undeniable vitality.

In 1976 Richter received a special award, the 'Golden Gramophone', from Polydor (owners of DG Archiv) for his achievements on record.

W. Neumeister/Deutsche Grammophon Production

FURTHER LISTENING

Bach keyboard music

The Goldberg Variations, BWV 988
These Variations – a form of composition not generally favoured by Bach – were originally published in 1742 with a long and cumbersome title. Their nickname derives from their association with J. G. Goldberg, a pupil of Bach's, who needed a composition to soothe his employer's sleepless nights. The music, though serene and undramatic, is hardly boring enough to send one to sleep, however! There are 30 variations in all, based on an earlier theme of Bach's, and it's worth pointing out that they are founded less on the theme itself than its accompanying bass – a musical construction typical of the mature Bach.

The Well-Tempered Clavier, Books 1 & 2
The two parts of this cycle come from widely separated periods. The first was completed in 1722, and the second compiled in 1744. They had come through a long gestation

period, and the perfection to be found in the vast majority of the 48 pieces demonstrates the fruits of this concentrated effort. The end result is one of the cornerstones of Western music: an inexhaustible collection which conveys a whole universe of musical ideas, concepts and feelings.

Musical Offering, BWV 1079
This work came about through King Frederick II's interest in music. Frederick had given Bach a theme on the clavier one day and comanded him to improvise a fugue on it. Bach had done this, but not to his own satisfaction. Consequently, on his return home, Bach set about writing this exhaustive set of elaborations on the King's subject. Of the 13 compositions making up the work, 10 are canons on the royal theme, one is a Trio sonata for flute – the King's instrument – and two are *ricercares* (an early type of fugue). The complexity of this work, especially the second ricercare, is extraordinary, and a great 'offering' to a cultured King.

LISTENER'S GUIDE

Orchestral suites nos. 2 and 3

Bach wrote four orchestral suites ignoring almost all the accepted rules to create diverse and wonderfully original pieces of music.

By the early 18th century, the orchestral suite was a well-established form. It had developed from the French overture (created by Jean-Baptiste Lully) and, in Germany, was popularized by composers of the stature of Telemann, Pachelbel and Buxtehude. An 'acceptable' suite was expected to include between two and four specific rural dance movements (the Allemande, Courante, Sarabande and Gigue) and to combine stately outer movements with a lively middle section.

But Bach could never do the ordinary. In the four suites of his that have come down to us, he wrote a total of only one Courante, one Sarabande and one Gigue, and he ignored the Allemande completely! On the other hand, he included at least one

Bourrée in all four pieces. Perhaps as a concession to more orthodox compositions, Bach called his suites *Ouvertures* and scored most of them for such a full orchestra that they could hardly hope to sound as rustic as a traditional suite would have done. As a result, the first movements are all in the accepted style of the French overture at that time (in France it was literally meant to be the opening to a theatrical performance). A show of stately pomp and ceremony (while the distinguished audience found their seats) is followed by a fugal-style movement (to give the soloists their chance) and, finally, by a return to the stately mood (before the curtain went up). It was Bach's particular genius, however, to contribute his unique flair for fullness of

Bach's orchestral suites are, in fact, French overtures, after the model of the 17th-century composer, Jean-Baptiste Lully (left). Lully's Ouverture, *written in a sparkling, courtly style, served as a 'curtain-raiser' to the French ballet-de-cour. The sovereign made his entrance to its stately strains, and then settled down to enjoy the dance suites that followed.*

Bach's orchestral suite no. 2 opens with a formal Overture – its solemn grandeur reflecting the mood of Bronzino's famous portrait of Eleanora di Toledo (right). Like Bach's music, Bronzino's painting is characterized by a restrained sense of opulence.

harmony and flashes of brilliant counter-point to this familiar form.

The writing of the Suites
It is not known quite when Bach composed his four suites, nor what his original instrumentation for them might have been. No original full score of the autograph manuscripts has survived and the parts we have may have been re-worked several times. Some of the parts of the second suite (written out by Bach for individual members of the orchestra), for example, do still exist and formed the basis for the first published edition (dated 1835). Various piano transcriptions of them became popular in the 1870s and 1890s, but these did not include all the movements.

The first three suites are only known in arrangements to accommodate the Collegium Musicum orchestra at Leipzig, where Bach was an honorary *Kapellmeister,* though research suggests they were originally composed for the little chamber ensemble he conducted at Cöthen – and it is this research which has influenced conductors like Neville Marriner (see page 53). As for the fourth suite, all that is known for sure is that in 1725, trumpets and drums were added.

Suite no. 2 in B minor (BWV 1067)
This suite is scored for a string orchestra (and harpsichord *basso continuo* accompaniment) together with a 'transverse' flute – that is, a genuine flute rather than a recorder. The implication is of a smallish ensemble, yet Bach was careful, when writing out the flute part of the first movement, to distinguish between solo and *tutti* (all together) sections, as if accommodating a larger orchestra. Either way, it is unusual to find that throughout the entire suite the flute always plays the melody, either as a solo or in unison with the first violins. It is never content to sit back and simply contribute to the harmony and, as a result, it is never given more than one rest!

Programme notes

The *Ouverture* is in the grand French style, a deliberate prelude to the light-heartedness of the country dances that follow. It is in three sections: a solemn beginning, a long, involved fugue and, finally, a return to the initial mood of stateliness.

The solemn opening statements are reinforced by the minor key; then, fractionally after the imposing chord introduced by the rest of the orchestra, the double trill of flute and first violins echo together. Indeed, trills abound: every instrument sports at least two within the first four bars – even the normally sombre basso continuo. As the opening movement advances, its mood lightens a little without losing its grand sense of occasion and a formal atmosphere returns at the close.

Suddenly, the flute and first violins

A. Bronzino 'Eleonora di Toledo'. Uffizi, Florence/Scala

The sixth movement of orchestral suite no. 2 is a Menuet. This dance, which was fast becoming a favourite in the courts of Europe, was traditionally of rustic origin. Watteau's painting captures the ambience – blending elegance with a pastoral setting (left).

This colourful and imaginative painting (below) echoes the light-hearted, 'flighty' nature of the finale. Bach called it Badinerie *('bantering'), expressing this idea through inspired and humorous scoring.*

proclaim the theme of a faster fugue. The second violins wake up and join in, beginning on a different note! The violas too make a non-conformist entry, in the original key, but an octave lower. Finally, the basso continuo – not to be outdone – makes its appearance in the same key as the second violins but copies the violas by choosing a lower octave:

Example 1

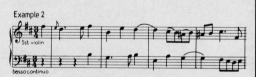

The theme is deceptively simple and is heard in fragments throughout the long development; the flute twists and turns through a series of solo episodes in which one, two or three other instruments chase anxiously after it in harmonic backing. A gathering crescendo finally results in the flute being caught and a mood of slow propriety is restored. Although the flute does escape the leash of the first violins for a couple more bars, it is soon restricted to playing in unison with them, and the movement draws inexorably to its close in what is, perhaps, a rather lugubrious overture.

The title *Rondeau,* which follows, is simply a way of saying that the major theme recurs at intervals, though each repetition may be separated by different music. This Rondeau is in the form of a gavotte, while the recurring theme is a charming and catchy little tune which is played once then immediately repeated. Elements of it also appear in the sections that fall between these repetitions, particularly among the second violins and violas. None of them is particularly lengthy – the longest being when the perky flute manages to slip in a solo above the violins –

and after these diversions, the rondeau theme returns and brings to an end this light, delicate movement.

Originally a Spanish dance with a very slow waltz-time measure, the *Sarabande* has seldom been so audaciously treated as here. Not only does Bach deliberately blur the rhythm – by introducing *grace* (optional secondary) notes on the beat, by holding the note before, on and over the beat, or even by replacing it entirely with a fractional rest – but the basso continuo treats the movement like a round, repeating interval for interval the violin and flute melody line. On top of that, the continuo starts on a different note! Much of this delightful mayhem is represented in the first four bars:

Example 2

In general, the second violins and violas are merely obliged to contribute to the harmony by adding their own attractive accompaniment.

The mood changes as another rhythmically blurred movement introduces a steadily paced *Bourrée,* reinforced by the basso continuo which plays a regular four notes per four-beat bar (repeating the same motif throughout). The first violins and flute are not so restricted, however, and their melody is every bit as memorable as some of the pieces composed by Handel. The second Bourrée in this movement features a solo flute and very subdued orchestra in contrast with the compact and determinedly forceful first. It really counts as no more than a quiet 'middle bit' before the first Bourrée is repeated and brings the piece to a rhythmic close.

After the Bourrée comes the *Polonnaise,* an ancient country dance from Poland which is in extremely slow waltz time. Resolute and stately, the second violins, violas and basso continuo impose a steady beat while the first violins and flute take the melody. The first two sections are for full orchestra and are repeated. The basso continuo then gives us a reminder of the tune while the solo flute plays in double time, harmonically fitting its melody above. There are no pauses or rests (so the flautist has to take breaths very quickly) and, as soon as this passage is over, the flute's stamina is tested further as it goes straight into a reprise of the full orchestral version.

Originally a rustic French dance from Poitou, the *Menuet* (or Minuet) in Bach's time was on the verge of becoming a favourite courtly dance. It was rarely set in a minor key, however, and Bach once again displays his innovative flair in the treat-

Understanding music: suites

The term 'suite' has been used to describe collections of many kinds, ranging from a retinue of servants, through a group of rooms leading from one to another, to a set of matching furniture. The musical suite shares similar features, with different movements having their own structure, function and place in the overall sequence, but linked together by the same musical ideas and the same key.

The basis of the instrumental suite was the dance. Most dances are in the first instance distinguished by their metre – whether they are duple, having two beats in a bar, or triple, having three. Additionally, they may be slow or fast, stately or sprightly. The idea of linking together contrasting dances goes back a long way, to around 1400. At first the slow, stately Pavan, in duple time, was paired with the fast triple Galliard, with elements of the same tune being adapted for both dances. Later, a third movement began to be added – either a Sarabande, a slow stately triple dance, or an opening prelude – which is not a dance, but a freely-designed movement serving to introduce the melodies and rhythms common to the dances which follow it.

Then, as now, fashions changed and new dances began to be introduced, especially at the French court where the dance tradition was particularly strong. The Pavan and Galliard were gradually replaced by the Allemande and Courante. The Sarabande gained in popularity, and was joined by the Gigue, a quick triple dance similar to the English jig.

Although French influence predominated, it was a German composer, J. J. Froberger, who is credited with forming these different dances into a regular pattern which, with various optional additions, formed the basis for the instrumental suites of Bach and Handel and prevailed until the suite itself was overtaken by the newer late-eighteenth century sonata form.

Froberger's suite was a cosmopolitan affair. It began with the Allemande, a slowish duple dance of German origin, followed by the French Courante, a quicker triple one. Next came the stately Sarabande, originally from Spain, and finally, the English Gigue. To this basic pattern a variety of optional extras were added, among them the Minuet, (as shown in the dance manual, right). Bourrée, Gavotte and Musette, and these additional dances fitted between the Sarabande and the concluding Gigue. Frequently the whole sequence was prefaced by a Prelude, and this was sometimes described in much more fanciful terms as 'fantasia' or 'overture'.

The suite also existed under various other titles. French keyboard composers grouped their pieces into Ordres, usually containing many movements each, while in Germany and Italy the term Partita was also used. In England a number of short simple suites were published by Purcell and Blow under the title of Lessons.

The suite reached the height of its development in the writings of Bach, who contributed not only the orchestral suites but also several for violin, for cello and for keyboard. The next generation of composers, however, turned their attention more towards the development of the symphony and the instrumental sonata. The idea of the suite remained in the Divertimento and the Serenade – both lighter kinds of orchestral pieces – but it was not until the later nineteenth century that the form began to reappear.

During the last hundred years the suite has re-emerged in a number of styles. With the growing interest in neo-classicism and the music of the past, some composers have turned back to the eighteenth century and re-created the baroque suite in modern dress – as in Ravel's 'Le Tombeau de Couperin' and Grieg's 'Holberg Suite'. Also, many composers have used the form of the suite to bring to the concert hall music originally written for the stage, either as incidental music to a play or for opera or ballet. Thus we are familiar with music from Bizet's 'L'Arlésienne', Grieg's 'Peer Gynt', Stravinsky's 'Firebird' and even Strauss's 'Der Rosenkavalier'. This last suite, with its emphasis on the music of the waltz which runs through the whole opera, brings us full circle to where the suite began – with music for the dance.

ment he gives it. The main characteristics of the movements are established from the start, as the first violin and flute take up the melody, and elements of their run-up to a high note occur throughout – especially in the melody-line. Both sections of the movement are repeated.

The next piece, *Badinerie* – which means something like 'bantering' – is probably the best-known movement of the suite and a favourite with concert flautists everywhere. With the Rondeau, it is certainly the most light-hearted and 'flighty' of

the entire collection (despite its minor key). Inevitably, the flute is given full rein, with the soloist in full command, and only the faithful basso continuo accompaniment has anything like the same amount of work to do. Even the first violins are reduced to mere harmonization, and are only granted the luxury of emphasizing the rhythm from time to time (though they do sneak in an occasional half-beat behind the flute's back!). To underline still further the flute's dominance, much of the string playing is *staccato* (very brief notes), particularly in

the second section. Both the complementary sections are then repeated in this gem of a movement, which requires considerable skill from the solo flute.

Suite no. 3 in D (BWV 1068)

This suite is scored for two oboes, three trumpets, a timpanist (with two kettle drums), two violins, a viola and basso continuo (cello and harpsichord accompaniment), though it makes light use of the wide selection. The oboes and trumpets, for example, never do more than reinforce

the violins or strengthen the melody line, though the trumpets still retain an individual and characteristic sound.

Programme notes

The regal *Ouverture* is in three sections: a stately beginning, a lively fugue and a return to slow solemnity, if not the original theme, at the end. From the beginning, the first violins, together with the oboes, dominate the melody line to such an extent that it is almost a recitative: the

Bach's orchestral suite no. 3 opens on a note of pageantry. The Ouverture moves solemnly forward like a regal procession (left), with trumpets and drums enhancing the ceremonial mood.

The Italianate Air – made famous through the arrangement Air on a G string *– contains one of Bach's most relaxed and expressive melodies. The music breathes a lyrical grace and tenderness (above right).*

Giovanni Bellini 'Madonna and John the Baptist' (detail). Accademia, Venice/Scala

nearest Bach came to putting mere chords beneath a tune. In the accompaniment by the second violins and violas, the classic 'dotted' rhythm (da-Da, da-Da) of the French Overture is quickly established:

This rhythm, constant through the entire first slow section, helps to promote an overall impression not merely of dignity but of formality and of regal ceremony.

Suddenly, the first oboe and first violins strike up the initial theme of a fugue. Shortly after their brusque interruption, the second oboe and second violins make their entry, followed at an appropriate distance by the violas and then the continuo. Trumpets and timpani do not participate in the fugue itself, though they provide underlying support. Their subordinate role continues as the fugal form breaks down and the first violins regain their dominance, revelling in the chance to overwhelm even their companion oboes and reduce them either to silence or to long-held notes of accompaniment. Their rule is briefly broken by a passage in

which everyone in the orchestra participates, before a combined statement of the opening theme brings this faster section to an abrupt close.

We are instantly back in high formality. The dotted rhythm reappears, yet the first violins seem uncharacteristically hesitant and are helped out by the trumpets in their one moment of real glory. Back on course, the string-led, recitative-like form is reasserted and once again the formal procession winds its way sedately to an end.

What an Italianate *Air* – a 'song' and not a dance at all – is doing in a suite is something of a mystery. Even stranger, it is a slow movement which comes straight after the equally slow end of the Ouverture, with little immediate impression of contrast. Yet contrast there is. Gone are the trumpets, oboes and timpani of the overture – the Air is played as a string trio with continuo accompaniment only. The piece incidentally achieved great popularity as a keyboard transcription, particularly the arrangement known as *Air on a G string*.

It is in two sections, both repeated: the first violin part carries the melody throughout and also includes some fairly long-held notes. From the beginning the continuo, too, establishes a very characteristic pattern in the bass – a progression of extremely rhythmic pairs of notes set an octave apart:

Example 4

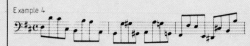

In the first section, the second violins
and violas are more concerned with
maintaining the harmony than with getting
in on the act. But there is already a hint
that, when the first violins are pre-
occupied with sustaining a longer note, the
second violins are at least prepared to
advertise their presence! This challenge is
taken further in the longer second section:
the continuo plods rhythmically on and,
almost every time the first violins have a
sustained note, the second violins definitely
compete and contrast, urged on by the
violas. The first violins never lose control,
however, and the movement winds in strict
order to a slow but majestic conclusion.

A *Gavotte* is a rustic French dance (the
name is Provençale for 'Alpine') but there
is nothing rustic about this movement,
scored as it is for the full orchestra
including timpani. Nor is it in the classic
two-section (binary) form. In fact, it is in
four sections, all repeated before the opening two are played through once more at
the end.

The movement starts brightly (and in
the classic manner) on the third beat of a
four-beat bar and the whole of this rather
short section seems to ask a 'question'
which the second then 'answers'. Typically
for Bach, the answer begins with an
inversion of the initial theme. The third is
put as yet another question, a longer more
formal one than the first, and begins with
every instrument playing in unison.
Between its busy passages, only a string
trio of violins and violas (together with the
oboes) carries the action and gives the
bustling continuo a chance to take a well-
earned rest. The question posed, the
answer follows (with no inversion this
time) and the trumpets are given rare
licence in some characteristically bright
fanfares before sections one and two round
off the movement as a whole.

It would be almost impossible to dance
to the following *Bourrée,* which is a piece
of Bach eccentricity based almost entirely
on an experiment in stressing the second
and third beats of a four-beat bar, without
stressing the first beat at all. The effect is
rather jerky – but catchy and stimulating
for all that. The trumpets, echoing the
violins (but playing an octave higher) are
elevated towards the top of their range,
whereas the basso continuo is once more
relegated to playing the rhythmic basis, far
from its prominence in the first and second
movement. The Bourrée is in true binary
form, however, with two sections that are
both repeated.

Taking its name from the medieval French
word for a fiddle, the *Gigue* is, traditionally, a light-hearted country dance
either to the sound of a fiddle or with the
dancers weaving from side to side (like the

Caterina dei Medici tapestry, Uffizi, Florence/Scala

The Gigue, like the Menuet, was originally a country dance, in this case to a fiddle accompaniment. Bach preserves some of its qualities in the lively violin melodies, but ringing brass and heavy timpani raise it to the level of a court celebration (left).

The pounding rhythm of the Gigue, entrusted to the basso continuo, seems to form a more suitable accompaniment to Domenico Tiepolo's tumblers (right) than to a light-hearted dance. However, its boldness inspires the music with confidence, bringing the orchestral suite no. 3 to a joyful conclusion.

G. B. Tiepolo 'Tumblers' Ca'Rezzonico, Venice/Bulloz

scraping of a bow). Bach's Gigue, however, is distinctly heavily scored: the trumpets and timpani, especially, pound away any pretensions to lightness and, although the classic, lilting 6/8 rhythm is retained, only the basso continuo is entrusted with it – and with mixed success: it is either lost amid the greatness of sound around it or seems clumsy to almost elephantine proportions:

Example 5

For all that, the movement is triumphant and bright, with a happy but contained sense of celebration. Both sections in its two-part form are repeated (the first as a question, the second as a much longer answer) and both make full use of the rhythm of the three long notes played at the very beginning. The second section is especially climactic; as the timpani rolls, the first trumpeter gradually builds to a supremely powerful crescendo and, with the oboes and first trumpet at the very top of their range, the suite comes to an ecstatic conclusion.

Sadly, many of Bach's orchestral pieces are lost to us and the surviving repertory can give only an incomplete picture of his genius: never mechanical, always inventive. The orchestral suites, at least, do justice to an outstanding composer.

Great interpreters

Neville Marriner

Neville Marriner and the Academy of St Martin-in-the-Fields have a long history of performing Bach's orchestral works. They are entirely familiar with the Suites and give clear, precise interpretations. Theirs are not, therefore, performances over-burdened with a large ensemble sound or with too much emphasis and gravity of feeling in the strings and brass. There are no clogged, muddy textures – a quality undoubtedly helped in today's recordings by advanced methods of music reproduction, which provide rich and full, yet vibrant and lively sounds.

Their performances do not use original instruments, but a 'period' spirit pervades their playing. The players catch the vitality of the music by performing it as accurately as possible. Particularly outstanding is the flautist William Bennet. His full and expressive tone, plus his assured and precise technique bring a completeness and balance to Bach's music. Marriner's conducting is always a discreet yet telling presence. He chooses tempos that are always just right: never so slow as to be dull, nor so fast as to make the music flow unnaturally. These insights into the correct playing of the pieces make the Academy particularly pleasing to hear.

Mike Evans

In the background

Scientists still argue which contributes most to our personalities, talents and behaviour: the inheritance of our genes or the influence of our environment. However, it is undeniable that we cannot help being affected to some extent by our surroundings, both in the narrow sense of our personal backgrounds and in the global sense of the times in which we live. Great composers are no exception, and the following pages describe the historical background to Bach's life and the political, economic and social events that influenced and inspired him: the career of Frederick II of Prussia, who combined enlightened despotism with military might to consolidate Prussian power in Germany and Europe; the explosion of world trade that brought 'new' products to Europe and sadly began the Atlantic slave trade; and the history of the plague which still haunted Europe when Bach was born, as it had done since the Black Death in the 14th century, but which began to disappear from Western Europe during Bach's liftetime.

IN THE BACKGROUND

Frederick the Great

Frederick II of Prussia, called 'the Great' (by his own subjects after the Treaty of Dresden in 1746), was one of those 18th-century rulers who are described by historians as enlightened despots. These monarchs – Frederick himself, Catherine the Great of Russia and Joseph II of Austria – were enlightened in that they patronized artists and writers and, to varying degrees, tried to put into practice the ideas of the philosophers of the Enlightenment in, for example, the codification of the law and economic reform. However, they were opposed to contemporary calls for political representation, and continued the methods of their absolutist predecessors, allowing their subjects little or no say in the running of the country. All the enlightened despots used their military power to try to expand the territories of their countries, and Frederick was perhaps the most successful: by the end of his reign in 1786, Prussia was without doubt one of the greatest powers of Europe.

In order to get a household of his own Frederick married Princess Elizabeth Christine of Brunswick-Wolfenbüttel (right), a shy woman who was devoted to him even though he had little interest in her. The newly-weds were given a charming country house at Rheinsberg (above). Here, Frederick was at last able to enjoy poetry, witty repartee, flute sonatas, wine and the company of fascinating foreigners without interference from his blustering father.

understanding that his way of life would never be unconventional enough to provoke his father. So although Frederick the Great was probably bisexual with his homosexual tendencies very much the dominant ones, he lived uncomplainingly with his dull wife and tried, unsuccessfully, to beget an heir. His father had promised him that he would be allowed to travel abroad once the succession to the throne was secure.

The years at Rheinsberg were to be a pleasant interlude in Frederick's life; the violence he experienced in his father's household was behind him and his own nature had not yet soured into bitter cynicism. Indeed he seems to have been motivated by a certain well-intentioned naivety, an idealism that would have made him snort with derision a few years later. He read a great deal and summed up his feelings and ambitions when he wrote to the Prince of Schaumburg-Lippe: 'Good intentions, love of mankind, and the hard work of a solitary can perhaps be beneficial to society and I flatter myself that I am not among its idle, useless members.'

An enlightened prince

In addition to Frederick acquiring a reputation for high-mindedness, he chose forms of relaxation that were a great deal more refined than those favoured by his oafish father. Every evening at Rheinsberg there was a concert unless the household performed a play. Chief performer at these concerts was Frederick himself who was an enthusiastic but somewhat erratic performer on the flute.

Witnesses conflict over Frederick's ability as a musician. He was certainly devoted to the flute and usually managed to practise for several hours every day. He also composed passably well and some of his pieces are still played, while his march 'Hohenfriedberg' is quite well known. On the other hand, many who heard him play recalled that his

music teacher, the composer Johann Joachim Quantz, coughed loudly whenever he played the wrong note and that this coughing was often rather frequent. Carl Philipp Emanuel Bach, who was recruited to the resident musicians at Rheinsberg as a cembalist, was said to have been literally tortured by his royal patron's dreadful playing. But plenty of disinterested members of his audience recorded that he was rather accomplished. Whatever the truth may have been, it is evident that music was a great entertainment and solace to Frederick throughout his life.

While he was crown prince Frederick was not rich but he was able to make modest attempts to patronize the arts. Many members of his household (in particular his cook) were French, and German was not used as a language by any of them. This arrangement, which would have provoked monstrous anger in Frederick William had he known of it, was at least partly in deference to the supremacy of French culture. Frederick was able to persuade the French painter Antoine Pesne to settle at Rheinsberg and he left many portraits of the crown prince and his small court. His favourite architect was the German soldier Georg Wenzeslaus von Knobelsdorff, who found his inspiration in the classic proportions of Ancient Greece.

This cultivation of the artistic side of life soon became known throughout Europe and Rheinsberg was visited by members of fashionable, international society, who would not have dreamed of staying at the court of the king of Prussia. As a final polish to the Rheinsberg idyll Frederick was able to begin a correspondence with François Marie Arouet Voltaire, the great sage of the Enlightenment.

'Your Humanity'

Voltaire's undoubted genius made him the most towering figure in contemporary European

Johann Joachim Quantz (above) was a composer and Frederick's music teacher. He improved the design of the flute, his royal master's favourite instrument.

Frederick was generally acknowledged to have been an accomplished flautist (above), although his timing was sometimes alleged to have been erratic. His compositions included flute sonatas (below), some of which are still played. In old age he lost too many teeth to be able to play and he consoled himself with an extra hour's sleep.

literature and a highly influential philosopher. Basically, Voltaire believed that tolerance and the exercise of humanity were both right and enjoyable, but he went rather further than earlier humanist philosophers had done because he ignored the traditional role of religion in morality. Indeed he was actively anti-religious, arguing that much cruelty and persecution sprang from religious bigotry. In addition to having these civilized ideals, Voltaire was a great wit whose sparkling conversation was famous and whose barbed plays and books had an enormous readership. Although he was highly honoured in France in his lifetime he was never to achieve a stable respectability because of his outspoken anti-clericalism and a rather sophisticated sex life, which was often considered immoral.

Frederick's unusually solemn opening letter to this brilliant Frenchman was siezed upon with delight. Voltaire had a number of little weaknesses of which snobbery and a rather grasping nature were among the most prominent. He was flattered to be sought out by a future king and, of equal importance, a king who would inherit one of the few full treasuries in Europe. He replied in terms of the highest praise and at a later stage· in the correspondence he hailed Frederick as a prince-philosopher, referring to him as 'Your Humanity' rather than 'Your Majesty'. It was out of the question for Voltaire to visit Rheinsberg – as he was both immoral and French it would have caused some act of wild violence by King Frederick William – but through his letters he exercised considerable influence over the young crown prince.

An indication of this was Frederick's own start in literary composition, which culminated in the celebrated *Anti-Machiavel*. In this work Frederick criticized the ruthless philosophy of the Renaissance theorist, Machiavelli, and argued that armed aggression was immoral and that duplicity would

In 1736 Frederick began his famous correspondence with the great French man of letters, Voltaire (above). Voltaire thought it a 'miracle' that 'the son of a crowned ogre, brought up with the beasts of the field, should understand the subtleties of Paris'.

serve a ruler badly. All in all, Frederick gave a convincing impression of a decent, civilized man of cultivated tastes whose reign was likely to be wise and peaceful. Yet it was vanity as much as his love of learning that drove Frederick on (he rather liked the image of himself as a philosopher and wit), and when he came to the throne, this same vanity would make him adopt a very different character.

The accession

When King Frederick William died in May 1740 a great restraint was removed from his oldest son. A ruthlessly executed separation from his wife was almost Frederick's first concern. His queen was expected to live at Berlin during the winter and at Schönhausen during the summer while Frederick moved to Potsdam and rarely saw her, behaving with the utmost coldness whenever he did. The new king also wrote to Count Francesco Algarotti, a handsome Italian philosopher whose best-known work was a popularization of Newton's theories on optics called *Neutonianismo per le dame,* begging him to join him as soon as possible.

Combining scientific knowledge with a love of art and music, Algarotti had been a welcome visitor to Rheinsberg and he was now briefly to become an intimate friend of Frederick's. However, it was soon apparent that the king of Prussia and his boon companion could not be absolutely carefree in their behaviour. On a pleasure trip to the French town of Strasbourg both men adopted aliases which failed to deceive the town's governor, the Marechal de Broglie. The governor managed to end the escapade in a humiliating way by sending for Frederick and offering to receive him with full honours. This was Frederick's only visit to the country he regarded as the centre of civilization.

But the complications of his unorthodox emotional life did not stop Frederick from bringing some humane reforms to his kingdom. He abolished the torture of civilians, decreed tolerance of all religions and allowed complete freedom of speech and expression by ending censorship. The Berlin Academy was reopened and the French philosopher, Pierre Louis Moreau de Maupertuis, was made its president on the recommendation of Voltaire. (The two Frenchmen professed to be great friends at this stage, though they eventually fell out because of Maupertuis's involvement with one of Voltaire's mistresses.) Frederick found Maupertuis amusing but lacking the brilliance of his rival, whom he now contrived to meet. In 1740 the new king of Prussia and Voltaire met in the Duchy of Cleves, enjoying a three-day 'honeymoon' in each other's company.

The seizure of Silesia

In those first months Frederick seemed set fair to become the enlightened monarch his inclinations promised but at the same time there were hints that he was, after all, his father's son. Upon his father's death, Frederick disbanded the famous Giant Grenadiers, a regiment of freakishly tall soldiers that had been Frederick William's pride and joy. But far from being a gesture against militarism, this was in fact an economizing measure of real benefit to the Prussian army because the money saved was used to raise 10,000 fresh soldiers of the line and to increase the supply of munitions. And soon the new king showed his true colours.

Within five months of his accession, Hapsburg Emperor Charles VI died leaving his family lands in

N van Blarenberghe 'Battle of Fontenoy' Versailles/Réunion des Musées Nationaux

Germany, Italy, Austria and Hungary to his young daughter Maria Theresa, as well as an agreement that her husband would be elected to his imperial title. All this had been solemnly ratified in treaties with the great powers, treaties to which Prussia was a signatory. However, Frederick's desire for the rich province of Silesia was so great and his longing for military glory so strong that he ordered his army into Silesia and siezed it from Maria Theresa. This started an episodic war which soon involved France and England and other German states, and which lasted, with long periods of peace, for almost two decades. The first round in the engagements ended for Prussia when Frederick faithlessly abandoned his allies and made a separate peace with Maria Theresa in June 1742. He had acquired all the territory he had gone to war for, a beautiful province about one-third the size of England, together with the reputation of a magnificent soldier and the character of an immoral cynic. 'Ambition, self-interest and the desire to hear my name spoken outweighed other considerations,'

On his accession Frederick disbanded the Giant Grenadiers, a regiment of super-tall soldiers (right) which had obsessed his 'drill-master' father.

the philosopher-king later confessed, 'and I decided for war.'

Far from feeling remorse, Frederick tended to revel in his new image as a hard-headed realist. His tendency to tease his chosen companions, to dwell on their weaknesses and to be disparaging about their motives became steadily more pronounced. But by 1742 these unpleasing characteristics were only beginning to develop and Frederick found it easy to attract the famous and artistic to his court as he turned his mind to the arts of peace.

Among the king's new friends was the Marquis Jean-Baptiste de Boyer d'Argens, whose passionate interest in painting and the theatre was infectious. He was made director of the Comédie-Française de Berlin. Pesne was commissioned to paint the ceilings of the palace of Charlottenburg and Knobelsdorff designed a fine opera house. Best of all, Frederick managed to attract Voltaire to Berlin, and the irascible Frenchman was so enchanted by the attention shown him – by the concerts, operas and things of beauty – that he proposed to make Prussia his permanent home. All this was most agreeable to Frederick but, in 1744, the dispute with Austria-Hungary flared up again and he was forced to

The Battle of Fontenoy (above) from the French point of view. Marshal Saxe, whose book on warfare was always by Frederick's bed, led the French forces to victory over the English at this battle in 1745. Fontenoy was a crucial fight in the long, episodic war that had started in 1740 after Frederick seized the Austrian province of Silesia. The Austrian empress, Maria Theresa (left), called Frederick a 'monster' but when she died in 1780 he claimed that though he had fought her, he had never been her enemy.

Frederick's dream palace at Potsdam, Sans Souci (right), was finished in 1747 and became his favourite home. Under the terraced greenhouses he grew the Mediterranean flowers and fruit that he loved.

mobilize his forces and, once again, go through the expensive business of making war.

Frederick in the field

By December 1745 the Prussian armies had gained enough crushing victories for Frederick to conclude another advantageous peace. His military reputation was very high indeed as he was an aggressive, confident commander who led the best equipped and most experienced force in Europe. In the kingdom of Prussia war was a deadly serious business for which the state was carefully prepared. Not all the great powers of Europe competed with quite the same dedication. The English tended to use their army as a holding centre for society's more violent misfits led by their most dangerous and least intellectual aristocrats, and the French frequently showed an insane adherence to outmoded concepts of chivalry.

Between them the French (who were Frederick's allies) and their English opponents mounted one of the 18th century's grimmer comedies at the battle of Fontenoy in May 1745. As the massed ranks of both sides approached to a lethal closeness, French and English officers capered about between the lines in an ecstasy of politeness, offering each other the honour of firing first. The English were quicker to tire of this pantomime and their grinning redcoats mowed down the French Guards with savage zeal. However, the last laugh lay with the French who won the battle handsomely; the English were so poorly led and badly trained that they were virtually incapable of large-scale manoeuvre – Frederick reckoned them and their commander no better than animals.

Great commander though he was himself, Frederick became less and less keen on fighting. As king of Prussia it was his habit to describe himself as the first servant of the state and it was evident enough that in most cases war was a damaging business for his people and country. At the end of 1745 he hoped that his territorial gains had been consolidated and

that his active military career was over. Once more he turned to building up his state and establishing a civilized way of life for himself.

The symbol of this lighter side of Frederick's life is the pleasure palace of Sans Souci (which translates as 'carefree'), which he and Knobelsdorff designed and built outside Potsdam. The pink and white building stands at the top of a slope, above terraces which are all glassed over so that they are reminiscent of a cascade. Frederick moved into Sans Souci in May 1747 and established an informal, almost entirely masculine court – the queen was never invited there.

The king now ran his life to a demanding schedule which made room both for long hours of work for the state and for his favourite diversions. He was always woken at 4 a.m., which he did not enjoy much, and his servants were instructed to throw cold water on his face if they found him dozing off. After he had enjoyed a brief musical session on the spinet, he turned to dealing with his voluminous mail. Next, he gave his day's orders to an aide and was ready by 10 a.m. to direct military exercises or catch up with his personal correspondence. He dined at noon and liked his company to be as entertaining as possible. In the afternoon he did administrative work and took exercises – usually a brisk walk. He practised the flute as much as four times a day which, despite his early start, ended late: supper was at 10 p.m. and this was usually followed by a concert.

It was an exhausting routine primarily dedicated to the service of the Prussian state and under this self-imposed slavery Frederick may well have felt himself entitled to his few hours of pleasure and entertainment. He imported wits, singers, actors, musicians and dancers to join his court. (The famous dancer Barbarina had a notable triumph in that she was reputed to have had affairs with both the king

The seductive Algarotti (above), to whom Frederick wrote when his father had died: 'I await you with impatience – don't leave me to languish.'

This Meissen centrepiece (right) was commissioned by Frederick in 1761. He was fond of fine porcelain and set up his own china factory at Berlin in 1763.

Sans Souci (left and far left) was a very personal palace where Frederick enjoyed the elegance that reminded him of Paris. Many of its interiors were decorated in the fashionable rococo style, which is characterized by the use of pale colours, including gold, mirrors, and naturalistic motifs such as clouds, foliage and birds.

Frederick's court was decidedly homosexual, for he liked to be surrounded by what one ambassador called 'he-muses'. The dancer La Barbarina (left) was one of the few women invited to Sans Souci.

and Algarotti.) Of his musical visitors the most distinguished was undoubtedly Johann Sebastian Bach who spent an evening at Sans Souci and later improvised a fugue on a theme given him by the king. While music was undoubtedly of great importance to the king, his chief pleasure was probably in witty conversation. But after all the promises and hesitations it was not until 1750 that Voltaire actually decided to make his home in Prussia. Once there, he and Frederick kept each other much amused for a short while until their relationship began to sour.

The Seven Years War

By 1756 Frederick was once more at war in the most disastrous, long drawn-out and desperate struggle of his reign. He was in the impossible position of fighting all the great continental powers at once with the English as his only allies. For this situation he could thank the misfiring of his cynical self-interest and his waspish wit. Maria Theresa had never forgiven him the robbery of Silesia and was able to make common cause with the king of France and the empress of Russia. Their hostility towards Prussia owed quite a bit to the stinging remarks which its king frequently made about them and which were freely reported to them. The English were delighted by the whole business and merely supported Frederick financially and with a minimum of troops while they overran France's overseas colonies.

The Seven Years War was a long torture to Frederick who was only just able to prevent the destruction of his state. His endless string of victories hardly dented the massive resources of his foes while his own army was constantly whittled away. Frederick's sombre letters to his friends reflect the nightmare he lived through in every desperate year until the death of the empress of Russia in 1762 dissolved the coalition against him. He survived this traumatic experience by 24 years but it left its mark on him, giving him an even sourer nature and a deep pessimism.

Frederick (centre) converses with Voltaire (in the lilac coat) and other cronies over dinner at Sans Souci. The king loved entertaining clever men and his visitors' accounts of him suggest that although he was capable of extraordinary rudeness, he was also a charming host in congenial company. Frederick the Great was always hardest on himself and was basically kind. As an old man he travelled extremely slowly in a battered carriage so as not to exhaust the elderly soldiers who formed his personal guard, and his last words were an instruction to his servants to throw a quilt over one of his dogs, which was shivering with cold.

Old Fritz

But this second half of Frederick's reign held achievements just as great as the military conquests and humane reforms of the early years. Prussia was able to flourish again after the ravages of the Seven Years War and she owed much of this to the tireless work of the man who became known as 'Old Fritz' to his people. He was very miserly over some things and became rather scruffy in appearance with his uniform covered in dog hairs and his boots unblacked. He drove himself hard with long hours of work, which he tried to continue into the last day of his life, and he was enormously popular with the Prussian people, although he always maintained that this meant nothing to him. At set times of the year he held

military manoeuvres or visited parts of his sprawling domains. In fact it was a pouring wet day at army manoeuvres that brought on the fever that eventually killed him.

After his death in August 1786 Frederick became one of the heroes of Germany, immortalized as a brilliant and resourceful soldier as well as a tireless and unbending servant of the state. His constant self-denial and disinterested humanity certainly made him a remarkable ruler by any standards. He was often coarse and had a vitriolic tongue yet the solace that he found in the arts showed his commitment to civilized values, and his enlightened stewardship of Prussia raised the standards of European government.

IN THE BACKGROUND

The growth of trade

Today, when supermarkets are full of exotic produce imported from distant lands, and when freezing and other food-storage techniques have abolished the seasons, it is difficult to imagine a world in which most people's diets were limited by what could be grown in the immediate area and the relatively few items that were imported. Trade has, of course, always existed: urban civilization probably began when people met to exchange their farmed produce for what they could not grow or make for themselves. And during the Middle Ages, Europeans travelled to the Far East in search of spices craved by the medieval palate. Indeed, the voyages of discovery in the late-15th and early-16th centuries began as a search for a quicker way to the 'Spice Islands'. Instead of spices, explorers brought back goods like tobacco and the potato. Sugar, coffee and tea also reached Europe at this time, and during Bach's lifetime, the growth of world trade transformed them from luxury items into staples of the Western diet.

IN THE BACKGROUND

'The wealth of the world'

Bach lived during an epoch of massive commercial expansion – a time when Europe's new found wealth could be lavished on exotic imports and 'wonder' foods such as coffee, sugar and tobacco.

P. Longhi 'Morning Chocolate' Ca'Rezzonico, Venice/Mauro Pucciarelli–Roma

France and Holland.

This enterprising new breed of merchants catered for an ever-expanding European demand for fancy goods and beverages like sugar, chocolate, tea and coffee which were fast becoming fashionable among the privileged classes. Just as the medieval world had craved spices and the Renaissance period saw the birth of a bullion market, so Enlightened Europe was developing a very sweet tooth.

The triumph of sugar
Sugar cane first found in India was carried to the Mediterranean and across the Atlantic to the tropical coasts of the Americas and the West Indies. Around 1680, sugar production in the Caribbean began to increase and, for the next 100 years or more, it rose steadily in response to a growing European demand. Sugar had advanced from being an exclusive rarity and was gradually becoming a commonplace item in most households. In 1800, for example, England alone used 150,000 tons of sugar a year – nearly 15 times more than she had consumed in 1700.

The demand for sugar had a knock-on effect that stimulated further trade in support of the Caribbean plantations. Growing cane left very little room for other crops, so food for the slaves (sugar growing was synonymous with slavery) had to be imported from other colonies or from the mother country.

Chocolate, tea, coffee and tobacco
Three new drinks – chocolate, tea and coffee – arrived in Europe at about the same time. Initially, they were used as medicines, then they moved into the 'luxury' market and, finally, became items of mass consumption in the cities.

Chocolate first arrived in Spain in the early 16th century – an import from her colony of Mexico. By 1659, when Louis XIV of France married a Spanish princess, it had become a favoured drink among the Spanish royal family. Within a hundred years the passion had been passed on to the French court and 'to go to the chocolate' meant to attend a royal levée. But, despite such distinguished patronage, chocolate never became as popular with the French as it was in the Spanish court.

The story of tea was rather more complicated. It first arrived with Portuguese, Dutch and English traders who had visited China. The popularity of this exotic new beverage was, however, inhibited by the need to import teapots and porcelain cups as well as the leaves themselves! (No other tableware was suitable for holding the delicate but hot liquid). The first cargoes of tea probably arrived in Amsterdam on

During the late 17th and 18th centuries, newly-formed trading links between Europe and the rest of the world strengthened into permanent commercial bonds that were to become vital to the prosperity of many nations. It was a time of massive commercial expansion and a time which saw the evolution of key business institutions and the beginnings of a modern consumer society. International trade was based along the Atlantic's east coast and, in the dynamic maritime countries of Holland, Britain and France, ports such as Amsterdam, Liverpool, London and Bristol, Nantes and Bordeaux were becoming the most important trading centres in the world.

The lure of long distance trade
Along with this flourishing trade came a new class of aggressive, self-assured businessmen ready to take advantage of the abundant profits to be made. Gold and silver from the Americas and exotic luxuries from the East had first lured merchants across the oceans and had been the stimulus behind the Spanish and Portuguese trading empires. But, by the mid-17th century, these trading systems had succumbed to the rising maritime power and influence of Britain,

The rise in trade in the 18th century promoted the growth of ports, like Bristol (left), across Europe.

Trade introduced new and exotic drinks like chocolate (above), which at first were the preserve of the few, then became the fashionable craze, and finally available to everyone to the extent that they became essential commodities.

As early as the 17th century, governments warned of the dangers of using the newly introduced tobacco – nevertheless the habit spread (right).

Fotomas Index

68

By the middle of the 17th century Amsterdam was recognized as the financial capital of Europe. The wealth of the country was founded on its seaborne empire, and the success of the Dutch East India Company. Its 'Bourse', or Exchange, was the centre of speculation and the model for similar institutions world wide.

ships of the Dutch East India Company in 1610, and from here part of the shipment found its way to England.

Indeed, it was the London of the 17th century that launched the fashion for tea drinking; Samuel Pepys records his first taste of it in 1660. But tea did not acquire mass appeal until the 1720s, when direct trade between Britain and China increased the supplies. By then, British trade was conducted from the few, restricted depots permitted in China itself and rising demand led to the creation of a veritable 'tea fleet'. Some historians have pointed out the coincidence of the first taxes on gin (1751) and the mercurial rise of tea as the 'national' drink. Certainly, the beverage seems to have done best in countries such as Russia and Britain, which were without the vine! It was some time before the government recognized the potential of this new tea-drinking craze but, when it did, they formally introduced a tax on the beverage which provoked the colonists of Boston, America to hurl chests of tea into the sea in their celebrated protest, the 'Boston tea party'.

Although tea enjoyed great popularity in both Britain and Russia, it never established itself to the same extent in either France or Germany. These countries took more readily to the third of the new beverages, coffee. By the 16th century, coffee drinking was widespread throughout the Muslim

world and it reached Vienna around 1615. From here it spread to Paris and then London. It was not until the end of the 17th century, however, that coffee became something of a national addiction – thanks in part to the appearance of chic Parisian cafés.

These cafés rapidly became a favourite meeting place for men of fashion and their patronage gave lasting respectability to the drink itself. In 1671, an enthusiastic French convert passionately listed the virtues of this new wonder drink.

It dries up all cold and damp humours, drives away wind, strengthens the liver, relieves dropsies by its purifying quality; sovereign equally for scabies and impurity of the blood, it revives the heart and its vital beat, relieves those who have stomach aches and have lost their appetite, it is equally good for those who have a cold in the head.

Within a hundred years all the citizens of Paris were equally enthusiastic; there was 'no bourgeois household where you are not offered coffee, no shopkeeper, no cook, no chambermaid who does not breakfast on coffee with milk in the morning'. Demand led to further trading centres; coffee grown in Arabia could not begin to satisfy Europe's craving and shrubs were transported to suitable new areas – Java (1712), Jamaica (1730) and Haiti (1730).

Between the 16th and 17th centuries tobacco grown in the New World was introduced to the Old World and soon enjoyed even greater popularity than tea or coffee. Its health hazards were recognized early on and the timing of government prohibitions on its consumption – England in 1604, Sweden and Denmark in 1632 and Russia in 1634, for example – mark the speed of its conquests. As history shows, these prohibitions were ignored and tobacco, taken as snuff, chewed or smoked in a pipe, produced such a profitable trade that on occasion it even outsold sugar. Tobacco had come to stay and, eventually, governments gave up trying to ban its use and instead exploited the revenue-raising potential it offered them.

The Dutch Pioneers
With such a buoyant market open to them, it is not surprising that 17th- and 18th-century merchants were more than ever prepared to undertake hazardous long voyages. Besides, such journeys were becoming more efficient and less costly because of the better design in sailing ships and improved charts and maps. The first nation to challenge the established Portuguese trade monopoly with the

East was Holland; its aggressively successful Dutch East India Company was founded in 1602. The company had sufficient power to negotiate direct with local potentates, to appoint admirals of the ships and the governors of trading depots, or 'factories', it used.

But the Dutch merchants had no intention of sharing the prizes they had wrested so competitively from the Portuguese. Up and coming traders who were not members of their élite company were prohibited from dealing in the seas east of the Cape of Good Hope or west of the Straits of Magellan. Even the Japanese, who had resisted previous contact with 'barbarian' foreigners, could not refuse them and granted the Dutch a strictly supervised trading centre at Nagasaki. Here, their officials enjoyed a luxurious but boring life 'dead and buried in an obscure corner of the globe'.

By the middle of the 17th century, the Dutch held sway over a huge commercial empire which provided Holland with all her needs. The small republic at the heart of this seaborne empire grew increasingly wealthy and powerful and Amsterdam became the financial capital of Europe. The whole city was well provided with warehouses and granaries 'from five to eight stories high', while houses alongside the canals had 'two or three store-rooms and a cellar'. Dutch towns were renowned for their learning as well as their commerce, and the canals that linked them were both an example of successful technology and a further stimulus to economic development. The affluent merchants of Holland displayed the rewards of their enterprise with fine clothes, country houses, yachts (the local equivalent of carriages) and a rich selection of paintings.

Britannia rules the waves

So formidable was the 17th century Dutch monopoly on Eastern trade that hopeful English and French merchants tactfully withdrew to India. Here, the supply of spices was less satisfactory, but this was offset by the availability of other valuable commodities such as calico and muslin, saltpetre and indigo. Although not the traders' first choice, India proved an excellent place for setting up 'factories'

In an attempt to raise revenue from its American colony, Britain placed a tax on imported tea. This was the last straw for the colonists who increasingly resented taxation by a government in which they were not represented. In Boston the townsfolk reacted particularly vigorously. Dressed as Indians, they protested by holding a 'Tea Party' and hurled 342 chests of tea into the harbour (right), rather than pay the tax due on them.

Having won the trade monopoly with the East, 17th-century Dutch merchants were not prepared to let anyone share their spoils. They were the only Europeans with whom the Japanese were prepared to deal, and were allowed to set up a luxurious trading post at Nagasaki (below). From here, strange and exotic goods were exported to an eager Europe.

70

and the coincidental collapse of the Mogul empire (which extended over a large part of the subcontinent) led to rapid territorial gains for the British East India Company.

British traders had gone to India as businessmen not conquerors but, by the mid-18th century, they found their factories (in Calcutta, Madras and Bombay) were well worth protecting against both French competition and local disruptions. When Britain and France were at war in Europe, their East India Companies were drawn into the conflict too and, in 1757, Robert Clive took possession of Bengal, after the battle of Plassey. With this defeat, the French steadily lost influence in India and Britain stood poised to take over the role of 'commercial power of the century'.

Trade routes

The most important of the great Eastern routes linked Lisbon with Goa and Macao; Amsterdam with Batavia (Java), Malacca, Sri Lanka and Nagasaki; and London with Surat, Madras and Calcutta. The round-trip to these destinations and back usually took at least two years. They were not simple two-way voyages, however; Europe's interest in the produce and workmanship of the east was not reciprocated: Asian countries demanded payment (in silver and copper) and this put European traders at a disadvantage.

To get around the problem, merchants generally engaged in local trading from 'Indie to Indie', shipping goods from one port to another – far from home but carrying on business that would make their ultimate journey possible. Their trade took them to many far-flung places; Persian silk was carried to India, sandalwood from Timor became a highly-prized currency in China and Chinese tea and porcelain were, in return, transported to Indonesia.

On the way home, European traders carried Indian textiles, Chinese tea, silk and porcelain, Sri Lankan cinnamon, Malaysian pepper, Moluccan nutmegs and countless other exotic products. The cargoes were sold at public auctions in Amsterdam and London for distribution throughout Europe and, in smaller quantities, to Africa and America.

Popular demand for these goods had somehow to

The new habit of drinking tea, coffee or chocolate created a demand for drinking vessels of the highest standard – and the practical yet exquisitely fine porcelain of China fitted the bill exactly. Before home markets could supply an adequate substitute or imitation, porcelain was one of the most valuable items of Eastern trade. Below, packers in China prepare a cargo of porcelain for transportation to England.

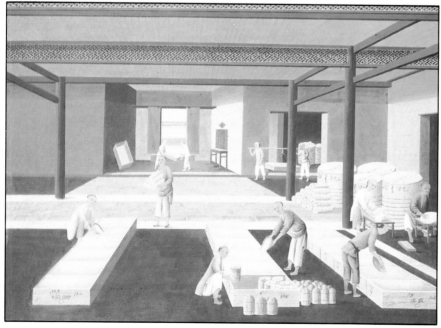

Robert Clive's victory over French and local troops, near a small Bengali village called Plassey, had momentous results. It secured for Britain valuable trading interests in India and consolidated her position as the greatest commercial power of the 18th century.

be met and led in turn to the development of improved inland communications. Dispersal throughout the various European countries was dealt with differently from place to place. In France, for example, people still focussed their attention on the twin attractions of land or the Court, rather than in dabbling in commercial enterprises, and internal customs barriers led to the concentration of capital in major towns or provincial areas, such as Bordeaux and Toulouse.

By contrast, England had no such restrictions and, though hampered by a lack of decent roads, her rivers and coastal lanes were in constant use. Shipping thrived and canal construction was twice as extensive as in France. These canals were built mostly to transport coal to centres like Liverpool and Manchester or, for example, manufactured goods from the Midlands, and the growing network stimulated fledgeling industries and growing towns that were to form an integral part of the industrial revolution.

Throughout Europe, there was a tremendous demand for the products of the East, on account of their delicacy, variety and technical perfection. Such

Europe's passion for sugar was one of the main reasons why slaves were imported into the Caribbean islands. Large numbers of workers were hauled in to work the canefields to meet the demand. It was in these canefields and other large plantations that the worst excesses of cruelty were perpetrated (bottom right).

was the infatuation with oriental textiles, for example, that in 1708, Defoe wrote scathingly:

... and even the Queen herself (Queen Anne) at this time was pleased to appear in China and Japan, I mean China silks and calico. Nor was this all, but it crept into our houses and bedchambers; curtains and cushions, chairs and at last beds themselves were nothing but calicoes or Indian stuffs.

In time, this infatuation led inevitably to imitation and with it came the industrial revolution – which started with the British cotton industry. The same story applied to porcelain: the taste for chocolate, tea and coffee made it necessary to produce wares that could supplement the greatly admired but costly, imported goods from China. Although European factories were quick to imitate oriental styles, they could not match the technical quality. Then, in 1708, a formula for porcelain (using Kaolin or china clay) was discovered in Germany. Within 50 years, porcelain factories producing fine 'china' had started up all over Europe. In due course, too, many of the countries which had sent handicrafts to Europe became prime markets for her industrially produced goods.

The slave trade

Behind the success of the Atlantic trade, especially the tropical produce and the silver and gold, and behind much of the commercial triumph, lay the shameful practice of slave trading. By the end of the 18th century, Britain was the main slave trader, though all leading trading nations were engaged in it to some extent.

The business was carried on by ships from Amsterdam, London, Bristol, Liverpool and Nantes. Cargoes of cheap cloth, guns, liquor and glass beads were exchanged for black slaves at trading depots on the Gold Coast and the estuaries of the Calabar and Niger rivers of Africa. Often dealing with African kings and merchants, they crammed their slave ships with from 200 to 600 men, women and children before clearing the 'Middle Passage' – the voyage across the Atlantic to the slaves' destination. With a good wind five in a hundred might die; in bad conditions about 30 or 40.

Sugar in particular needed huge numbers of unskilled, easily supervised workers and the slave populations of sugar-producing regions grew in accordance with Europe's passion for the food. On the sugar plantations of the West Indies and Brazil, the tobacco and rice plantations of the southern American colonies and the silver mines of Mexico, these captured Africans laboured in regimented gangs. Perhaps because the commercial advantages of the trade were so overwhelming, little protest against this inhuman practice was made much before 1750. Even in the cities of Europe, black slaves were common – slavery was still legal in Britain until 1772 and the trade itself was not abolished until January 1808.

Other major trade routes were transatlantic: from London, Bristol and Liverpool, to Boston, New York, Charleston and Kingston; from Lisbon to Recife and Bahia; from Seville and Cadiz to Vera Cruz and Havana; from Rouen, St Malo, Dieppe and Nantes to Quebec, New Orleans and Martinique. But, unlike the Asian trade, only raw materials were sought in return for European produce. For weapons, salt beef and wine, for example, the old world gained sugar, rice, silver, gold, hides, furs, fish and timber. In average conditions, the Atlantic could be crossed in

As the leading commercial power Britain was also one of the most notorious slave trading nations. Hundreds of men, women and children were stacked into slave ships (below) and taken from their African homelands to destinations in Europe and the New World. Many died on the way.

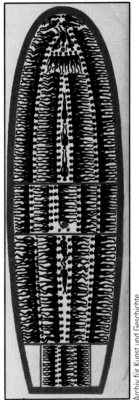

Archiv für Kunst und Geschichte

Michael Holford

Crown Copyright. Courtesy of the Library, Royal Botanic Gardens, Kew

one or two months. Winter sailings were avoided as much as possible and a ship was not normally expected to complete more than one round trip in a year.

Stock markets and speculation

Innovative financial practices and institutions had to evolve to meet the needs of the enormous growth in international trade. One clear sign of the times was the exchange and stock markets that developed in major financial centres such as Amsterdam and London. The stock exchange, or bourse, was the meeting place of bankers, merchants, exchange currency dealers, brokers and the like.

The great building of the Amsterdam Exchange was finished in 1631 and some 4,500 people crammed into it every day during the short business hours from noon to two o'clock. It was an immensely noisy and confusing scene, like a continuous funfair, yet speculation reached a degree of sophistication and abstraction which made it a very special trading centre. Here, government stocks and prestigious shares in the Dutch East India Company were prime targets for speculators and an expert could make a comfortable living simply by judicious betting on share prices. Something altogether new and 'modern' had happened: the fluidity of the market,

Flourishing transglobal trade led to the introduction of many new plants to countries where they had been completely unknown. In this way, maize (above), was carried to Spain and the Balkans and its ready adaptation to local conditions had a lasting effect on the domestic economy of these areas.

The increase in trade had a great effect on internal communication in many countries. To cope with the distribution and export of goods, new and better roadways had to be developed and whole new road network programmes were started. Mid-18th century France boasted a network of superbly built roads (right). At first Britain lagged behind – the pitted tracks that served as highways were described as 'more like the retreat of wild beasts and reptiles, than the footsteps of man'.

Joseph Vernet 'Building a Main Road'. Louvre, Paris/Giraudon

the publicity and excitement attached to it and the freedom of transactions had never been experienced before. In Amsterdam, frenetic gambling sometimes reached bizarre lengths. In 1634, for example, a 'tulip mania' swept the country and a bulb of no intrinsic value could be exchanged for 'a new carriage, two grey horses and a complete harness' – such was the desire to keep up with the fashion.

Outside stock exchange hours, the speculators and brokers (and small savers who were denied access to the inner sanctum of the exchange) gathered in the new *coffy huisen* (coffee houses) 'with their welcoming stoves and tempting pastimes; some offer books to read, others gaming-tables and all have people ready to converse with one; one man drinks chocolate, another coffee, one milk, another tea and practically all of them smoke tobacco . . . In this way they can keep warm, be refreshed and entertained for little expense, listening to the news . . .'

The London stock market

London soon imitated Amsterdam and, by 1695, the Royal Exchange was seeing its first transactions in public stock and shares. The exchange attracted those who 'having money already, wished to own more, as well as of the more numerous class of men

who having nothing, hoped to attract the money or those who possessed it'. The fledgeling stock market soon found itself cramped for space, however, and by 1700 it had moved across the road to Exchange or 'Change Alley'.

As a result, the coffee houses of 'Change Alley, like their counterparts in Amsterdam became centres of intrigue, speculation and power. The share brokers and public stock brokers refreshed themselves at Garraway's and Jonathans; specialists in maritime insurance went to Lloyd's and the fire insurance men went to Tom's or Carsey's. Despite this enthusiasm, financial institutions were still unstable – partly because the government tended to draw on them for credit and partly because investors panicked easily; many were ruined by the notorious South Sea Bubble crisis of 1720. The collapse of the South Sea Company, upon which heavy speculation had centred, led to a change of government and the Bubble Act of 1721, which forbade the formation of joint-stock companies without a royal charter. But further disaster was looming; in March 1748, the whole bustling district of Exchange Alley was destroyed by fire. In 1773 a new building was put up, behind the Royal Exchange. It was called the Stock Exchange.

Trade and power

To the merchants and brokers of the 17th and 18th century, it must have seemed that a world of never-ending profit and luxury was within their grasp if only they could make the right moves at the right time and if their governments were sympathetic to their needs. But the traders were businessmen first and foremost and wholly pragmatic in their attitudes towards their trading partners in the non-European world. Although trade on the scale reached in the early 18th century did require European settlements around the world (to provide facilities such as

The collapse of the South Sea Company, in 1720, exposed the fragility of the new financial institutions and inspired satirical reviews in the popular press of the day (left). The company, founded on genuine speculation over profits to be made in South America and the Pacific, became so buoyant that it even took over the whole of the national debt, except that owed to the East India Company and the Bank of England. Investors were persuaded to exchange state annuities for company stock and, when prices fell, many were ruined.

74

Sumptuous new fabrics and materials from the East became fashionable among 18th-century Europeans. Wealthy men and women basked in the surroundings of exotic imports – fine carpets and fabrics, aromatic spices, precious stones and metals – and, of course, slaves.

warehouses and ports, as well as contacts), the traders were not interested in direct rule. As long as economic loss was minimized, people were not concerned about losing colonies; after the American War of Independence, for example, the British government maintained a healthy trading relationship with its former subjects. It was only much later, in the 19th century epoch of imperialism, that European international commerce began to demand captive overseas markets.

The rise in the volume of international trade also worked to the advantage of people who had never even set eyes on a trading ship. The most startling spin off was the vast impovement in diet facilitated by the new trade and generally improved communications:

Upon the whole, to sum it up in a few words (wrote Daniel Defoe in 1728), *Trade is the Wealth of the World; Trade makes the difference between one Nation and another; Trade nourishes Industry, Industry begets Trade; Trade dispenses the natural Wealth, which Nature knew nothing of; Trade has two Daughters, whose fruitful Progeny in Arts may be said to employ mankind; namely Manufacture and Navigation.*

IN THE BACKGROUND

Europe and the plague

In 1348 Europe was struck by a terrible illness. Brought from the East by Italian sailors, it spread with alarming rapidity and virulence, and by the end of 1350 one-third of the population of Europe was dead. This terrible scourge was the Black Death, and in various forms it returned to terrorize Europe during the next 400 years. The plague was truly terrifying since there seemed to be no cure and no way of preventing the spread of infection (contemporaries did not realize that the bacillus was carried by fleas living on rats). This unexplained scourge continued to be an ever-present danger to European society until the 18th century when it began to disappear. Until the general improvement in public health and the development of modern drugs, other diseases like typhoid, smallpox and cholera continued to haunt Europe, but none was as deadly or as generally feared as the Black Death.

IN THE BACKGROUND

'Bring out your dead'

During Bach's lifetime the terrible and recurrent plague struck parts of Europe several times – seemingly dealt out as acts of divine retribution.

In the year of Johann Sebastian Bach's birth, 1685, a cycle of plague that had swept through Austria and Germany was nearing its end. In Vienna, 76,000 people had died in 1679. In the town of Halle, near Leipzig, half the population of 10,000 perished in 1682. Yet these stark figures show only a drop in the ocean of dead left by the unrelenting terror and havoc of plague in the 17th century. Throughout Europe people lived with the sheer horror of a disease that would wipe out whole communities with one fatal blow and which could mysteriously strike again at any time.

Yet it was during Bach's lifetime that the plague began to disappear as a major killer in Western Europe. A few more outbreaks – in Hamburg in 1713 one sixth of the population was wiped out, and about 40,000 people died during the plague of Marseilles in 1721 – lingered on to remind Europe of the savage virulence of this disease. And then it was gone. Plague continued to recur in the Balkans and Russia throughout the 18th and 19th centuries, but in western Europe people gave thanks to God for deliverance from a disease that perpetrated a reign of terror spanning four centuries.

Arrival of the Black Death

It began with a headache and a rising body temperature. Dizziness and intolerance to light were also common symptoms. After two days the temperature soared to 106°F and the patient became dazed, with slurred speech. But the first specific signs were the buboes – inflamed glandular swellings that usually appeared in the groin or the armpit. The excruciating pain seemed to be tearing the body apart as the buboes turned to pus and opened outwards – then death usually occurred within six days. The cause of the unpleasant end was bubonic plague, or the Black Death as it was called when it first arrived in Europe from China in the 14th century.

In 1347 the armies of the Mongol prince Kipchak Khan were besieging Caffa, a fortified town in the Crimea which was a trading post used by Genoese merchants to do business with the East. But the siege was disturbed by the sudden outbreak of plague among the Mongol army. They decided to end their military operation, but as a parting shot they put diseased bodies into giant catapults and lobbed them over the walls into the beseiged town. The Genoese tried to dispose of these lethal bodies as fast as they arrived, but the plague was too virulent. It established itself in the town, and the Italians in a panic took to their boats and left the Crimea for

Domenico Gargiulo 'The Plague of Naples' National Museum of Charterhouse of S. Martino, Naples/Luciano Pedicini

Europe, bringing bubonic plague with them. By the spring of 1348 the disease had established itself in Sicily and the south of France, then it tore through Europe like a whirlwind of death in just three years. By 1350 it had reached Sweden and Finland, and behind it a third of Europe lay dead. No other disease or war had devastated Europe on such a scale.

One reason why the plague was so lethal was that it was changing its form as it spread. Bubonic plague, characterized by swellings, is the archetypal plague. The fatality rate was between 60 to 90 per cent and death occurred within a week. It was a particularly unpleasant form of death in which the body of the victim appeared to shrivel up and rot: as one French chronicler put it, 'All the matter which exuded from their bodies let off an unbearable stench; sweat, excrement, spittle, breath so foetid as to be overpowering; urine thick black or red.

St Rock (right), the patron saint of plague, nursed the sick when the Black Death hit Italy in the 14th century. Legend has it that he healed victims using supernatural powers until he himself was stricken.

Plague and pestilence – an ever-present threat to Europe for over 400 years. Its cause unknown, people naturally assumed that the whirlwind of death and destruction was the hand of God, striking out at their sinful and errant ways. The terror it held is evident in the many paintings of plague outbreaks, and these appear almost like icons – reminders to tread a devout path in life, lest God wreak a terrible revenge. In the painting of the plague of Naples (left) galley slaves were forced to drag corpses along the street and on to carts using long hooks to avoid touching the victims.

With no defences to put up against the plague, its arrival was apocalyptical. It is hardly surprising, therefore, that the people of the time felt totally impotent against such powerful forces where Death (right) rode and raged at will – and triumphed.

Although nothing known could cure the plague, various medicinal potions and herbs were advocated as remedies or protectives against infections. The illustration (below right) symbolizes the effectiveness of two such herbs.

This alone seems bad enough, but unfortunately bubonic plague was also capable of mutating into pneumonic plague. This form was much more infectious and even more lethal. A modern study of pneumonic plague carried out in Manchuria in 1924 concluded that recovery was virtually unknown and that life expectancy for victims of pneumonic plague was 1.8 days. The reason that this form was more infectious was that it arose when the plague victim had a secondary infection of pneumonia – every cough and sneeze released thousands of plague bacilli into the air where they could be breathed in by the next potential victim. It is this form of the plague that is remembered in the children's nursery rhyme:

'Ring a ring a roses
A pocketful of posies
Atishoo! Atishoo!
We all fall down.'

A third and even faster form of the plague also appeared during the Black Death. Today it is described as septicaemic plague as it primarily attacks the bloodstream: within a few hours the blood is swarming with a particularly infective form of the plague bacillus. Records from the time speak of some victims who went to bed, healthy and cheerful and simply never woke up. Septicaemic plague had

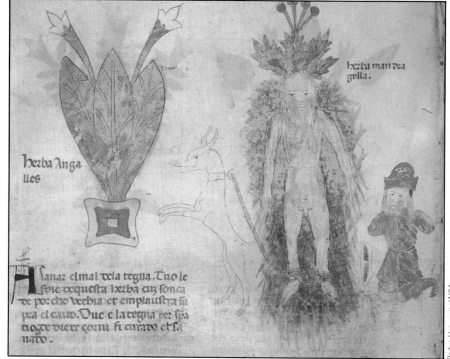

killed its helpless victims in a few hours overnight.

Despite thousands of years of contact with humans, the effects of the plague had not been diluted. In fact, the extraordinary thing about the plague was the virulence of its bacillus – the bacteria that causes the disease; it was capable of killing 90 per cent of the people it encountered.

If the disease had afflicted only people, it would probably have exterminated itself by wiping out its host. However, humans were only incidental to the career of the bacillus responsible for the plague.

The bacillus is carried by large, burrowing rodents (in plague time these were the black rats that infested most European cities) and the fleas that live on them. The infected fleas would bite humans and transmit the disease with devastating results.

The wrath of God

Of course the idea that a single disease which could assume at least three different forms was working its way through Europe was incomprehensible to the 14th century mind. All people knew was that unbelievable destruction was all around them, so they sought an explanation and a scapegoat. The explanation was usually the wrath of God – an idea that was to raise its head with every subsequent plague epidemic, right into the 17th century. And the scapegoats in Europe at this time were usually the Jews. A few other unpopular groups – for instance, the Arabs and the lepers – also had to endure some suspicion and some attacks, but they were usually vilified as the agents of the Jews who were regarded as the masterminds behind the poisoning of wells all over Europe.

British Museum/AISA

The Mansell Collection

Throughout Europe, though particularly in strongly Catholic countries, such as Spain, scapegoats were sought to blame for the plague. The Jews (above) were frequently the target and suffered many massacres as a result.

Plague doctors administering to victims wore strange protective clothing (left). Covered from head to toe in leather, the garb was capped with a mask with glass eye-holes and a long bird-like beak. The beak contained aromatic herbs to ward off infections.

In Basle, all the Jews were herded into wooden sheds and burnt alive. In Strasbourg, a large and prosperous Jewish community of about 10,000 people was exterminated. Similar attacks took place in Spain, Flanders and Germany. By 1351, the plague was on the wane, and so were the attacks on the Jews – however about 350 massacres had taken place.

Widespread panic

Having established itself in Europe, the plague hung on and erupted periodically as epidemics. Recurrences of the plague were recorded in the 15th and 16th centuries, but its final ravages during the second half of the 17th century were among the most lethal and also the best documented.

As soon as the plague had established a grip on a city the better-off citizens fled. This is something common to all accounts of the plague in Europe, and to this extent the hardest hit were the ordinary people rather than the wealthy merchants and the aristocracy. In Avignon in the 16th century, for example, landlords would write into the leases of their farm property that they had a right to take shelter there if the plague should break out in town. In the Savoy region of France, rich people would install a peasant woman in their house after the plague had subsided, as a guinea-pig to test (at the

Isolation of the infected was a major problem whenever the plague broke out. Medical knowledge was very scant indeed; and hospitals (left), or the more segregated 'Pest-houses' were ridiculously few and far between and usually over-crowded – often with two to a bed.

Although no medical understanding existed of the precise link between the appearance of the plague and rats and fleas, the connection was obviously noticed as the picture of the plague-ridden body swarming with rats and fleas (below) shows.

risk, of course, of the peasant's life) whether or not the danger was really over.

A considerable exodus also occurred in London during the Great Plague of 1665. Many of the well-to-do moved to the country or at least the 'safer' environs of London. However, a few notable characters, such as the famous diarist Samuel Pepys, felt that they could not desert their home town, and it is through such men that we now have a very clear picture of what life must have been like not only in the plague-stricken London but in many 17th-century European towns and cities.

Pepys, for instance, moved his wife to lodgings in Woolwich, but nothing could prevent him continuing to live and work in London – as an Admirality official he was, after all, busy running the war against the Dutch as well as keeping his diary. In response to a friend's concern for his well-being and safety he replied, 'You, Sir, took your turn at the sword: I must not grudge to take mine at the pestilence.' A very courageous statement indeed, but Pepys never tried to hide the dismay he felt at living in a town he considered 'distressed and forsaken':

'. . . I having stayed in the city till about 7,400 died in one week, and of them about 6,000 of the plague, and little noise heard day nor night but the tolling of bells; till I could walk Lumber Street and not meet twenty persons from one end to the other, and not fifty upon the Exchange; till whole families (ten and twelve together) have been swept away; till my very physician, Dr. Burnet, who undertook to secure me against any infection (having survived the month of his own being shut up) died himself of the

*plague; till the nights (though much lengthened)
are grown too short to conceal the burials of those
that died the day before, people being thereby
constrained to borrow daylight for that service;
lastly, till I could find neither meat nor drink safe,
the butcheries being everywhere visited, my
brewer's house shut up, and my baker with his
whole family dead of the plague.'*

Probably the best record of the effect of the plague
on a European city is Daniel Defoe's *A Journal of the
Plague Year* (which was in fact written in 1720). He
describes how the King and the court departed for
Oxford in 1665, leaving London to a skeleton
governing service and to quack doctors who
advertised 'Never Failing Preservatives against the
Infection. Sovereign Cordials against the Corruption
of the Air. Anti-Pestilential Pills.'

Anyone who could avoided London at all costs.
The farmers and market gardeners still plied their
trade, but to avoid contagion they came no further
than the fields surrounding the city, such as
Spitalfields, and withdrew as soon as they had
collected their cash.

According to Defoe, at the height of the plague, all
order seemed to disintegrate as panic spread:

*'It is scarce credible what dreadful Cases happened
every Day. People in the Torment of their Swellings,
running out of their own Government, raving and
distracted, throwing themselves out of their
Windows, shooting themselves. Mothers murdering
their own Children in their Lunacy; some dying of
mere Fright and Surprise without any Infection
at all.'*

Wherever the plague hit, whether in Britain or in
Europe, there were outbreaks of religious mania.
Plague was still seen as a sign of divine wrath, so
processions of sinners – sometimes indulging in self-
flagellation, or making pilgrimages on their knees –
would wend their way through the deserted streets.
In Catholic countries, Masses were celebrated at
street corners while the congregation participated
from behind their shuttered windows.

Living alongside the plague

Some cities improvised a public health service.
Because no one knew exactly how the disease was
caused, the most widely held theory was that the
plague somehow resulted from a corruption of the
atmosphere. Accordingly, special plague doctors
adopted a protective attire. The shirt and trousers
were made of skin and covered by a long robe. A
strange mask fitted over the face, from which a bird-

*After sunset, the sound
of the plague bell could
be heard in the streets,
and cries of 'Bring out
your dead' heralded
the arrival of the dead-
cart (below). Houses
that had been 'visited'
were shut up, and red
crosses and the words
'Lord have mercy on
this house' were
painted on the doors of
infected households.*

J. E. Delaunay 'The Plague in Rome'. Louvre, Paris/Bulloz

During the 17th century the plague was referred to as the 'Visitation'. In this allegorical depiction of Almighty power – the angel of death comes knocking at the door (left).

Rules concerning the burial of the dead were strictly adhered to – if with somewhat irreverent regard for the bodies. No family or friends were allowed to be present. The bodies were sprinkled with quicklime and unceremoniously tipped into pits (right).

like beak protruded, containing strong-smelling chemicals to combat the prestilential vapours that were thought to be wafting through plague-ridden communities.

In London, with the court and parliament safely settled in Oxford a new local government was swiftly drafted into action. A growing knowledge that no medicine could eradicate the plague meant that attempts at quarantine had to be made (the hospitals and pest-houses, for what they were worth, were ridiculously over-crowded). Firstly, no one could travel without a certificate of health and all unnecessary journeys were prohibited.

Other orders included: 'Notice to be given of the Sickness'; 'Sequestration of the Sick'; 'Airing the Stuff'; and 'Shutting up the House' to name just a few. All houses that had been visited – the plague was often referred to as the Visitation – were shut up for 40 days and a red cross was painted on the door, along with the words 'Lord have mercy upon us!'. After the 40 days were up, a white cross was painted on the door and was left there for a further twenty days as a warning to potential lodgers. The house was 'fumed', washed and whited with lime. No clothing or household goods could be removed for three months.

The disposing of bodies was a particularly strict procedure:

'That the Burial of the Dead by this Visitation be at most convenient hours, always either before sunrising and sun-setting, with the privity of the Church-wardens or Constables, and not otherwise; and that no neighbours nor friends be suffered to accompany the corpse to church, or to enter the house visited, upon pain of having his house shut up, or being imprisoned.'

At the plague's peak the only way to cope with the thousands of dead was to pile the bodies unceremoniously into mass graves. Graves had to be at least six feet deep, and in London massive pits were dug. One public grave in Aldgate was 40 feet long and 20 feet broad – big enough for about a thousand bodies. Corpses were treated with quicklime to speed up the rotting process.

Orders were also released for cleansing and keeping the streets 'sweet'. Every householder was responsible for sweeping the street outside his house every day. And any animals found roaming were instantly killed. There were laws, too, regarding 'loose Persons and idle Assemblies'. No wandering beggars were to be suffered in the city; all plays, bear-baiting, games and singing of ballads were prohibited. In fact, every form of entertainment was severely curtailed: 'That disorderly Tippling in Taverns, Ale-houses, Coffee-houses, and Cellars be severely looked into as the common Sin of this time, and greatest occasion of dispersing the Plague'.

An Examiners' Office was set up in each parish: three Examiners were to ascertain which houses had been affected by the plague, and to each house they assigned two Watchmen – one for day and one for night. The duty of these Watchmen was to prevent anyone visiting an infected house – or, indeed, that those shut up were not allowed out. The healthy of the household were confined along with the sick – the idea being that the plague was so catching that anyone who had been in contact with a plague victim would surely be stricken himself, and was therefore a danger to the public. Many escapes, however, were made when the Watchman was sent on an 'errand'. One writer of the time described how in desperation people fled from their houses, leaving their families

Guildhall Library

Although parish registers of deaths were sometimes haphazard and inaccurate – it only takes a glance at the one above to see the devastating effect of the plague on the weekly figure in a small community.

to the care of the parish. They would run as far away from their homes as they could:

'See, see, we infect not our next neighbours, and this sickness spreads not so much in any one place, but we carry it from place to place, running from our home as from our places of torment, and thus the roads are visited, and men travel the same way to the country and to their long home. Thus the contagion hath reached most places round the city, which is now as it were "beseiged".'

Keeping a true record of deaths and the cause of deaths was rather a hit and miss affair in 17th century London. So each parish appointed Women Searchers who were to be 'of honest reputation and of the best sort as can be got in this kind'. The unenviable job of these women was to visit every sick person in the parish and to report which of them had died of the plague. No Searcher during her time of employment was allowed to keep a shop or stall, or to work as a launderess – in effect the women, who were always from among the very poor, were treated as outcasts. So, too, in a way were the Nurse-keepers, the Watchmen, the Buriers – all carried a red rod of at least three feet long so that they could be identified. They were not allowed to go into any home other than their own and had to live an isolated life.

Defoe recorded numerous instances of bribery and corruption as panic and incipient hysteria mounted. Some people whose houses had been closed up by the authorities would bribe their way out. On the other side of the coin, there were 'wicked instances of Nurses' and Watchmen who attended infected people using them barbarously,

The plague was finally and dramatically wiped out of London by the Great Fire of 1666. A new building programme was started soon after and was used extensively to replace the burnt wooden buildings. This improved domestic hygiene and living conditions generally and resulted in fewer rats occupying the city. This in turn helped to prevent further plague epidemics.

Mary Evans Picture Library

starving them, smothering them, or by other wicked means hastening their End'. A great many robberies took place in the houses of the sick and the dead.

Europe recovers

In Britain, the plague died down in the winter of 1665 but welled up again, spreading to other parts of the country, in the following two years before finally vanishing forever in 1667. The detailed records show that at least 70,000 people died of the disease – one sixth of the population of London at the time.

Some historians argue that one factor in the withdrawal of the plague from London – and from western Europe as a whole – was the way in which stone, tiled buildings were beginning to replace wooden, thatched ones. At the root of the plague was, of course, the chain of contact between rats and fleas and people. Rats were endemic in wooden buildings, and were particularly associated with thatched roofs. Infected fleas from host rats could easily drop out of the thatch on to occupants or passers-by, and this could trigger off a plague epidemic. After the 17th century, plague persisted in the Balkans and in parts of Russia, where wooden buildings and thatched roofs remained common. Others have argued, however, that the plague also

withdrew from towns which did not experience a massive re-building programme – as London did after the Great Fire of 1666. It is also said that plague epidemics display a life-cycle of their own and that they can well up and subside without any help.

The early part of the epidemic that swept through Germany and Austria – and which continued to rage until just before Bach was born – had coincided with the Thirty Years War. It was not the fighting that had taken the heaviest toll, but the plague, typhus and famine that followed behind the armies like a tail of a comet, and reduced Germany's population by seven million. Once the epidemic was over a slow recovery started at once: the population rose back to its previous level by the time of Bach's death in 1750.

Europe was beginning to enjoy the fruits of exploration. Trade was booming and more and more people were getting used to a higher standard of living. Better social conditions meant less disease. With a new awareness of health and hygiene that appeared – albeit a very basic one – some of the old diseases, such as plague and leprosy vanished from western Europe, while other ceased to be epidemics which could wipe out half the population. This change not only laid the basis for the sharp population increase of the next century, it was also an important factor in the rise of Europe.

The macabre origins of the popular children's nursery rhyme 'Ring a ring a roses' dates back to the time of the plague. The first part refers to the carrying of flowers and aromatic herbs as protection against pestilential vapours. 'Atishoo! Atishoo! We all fall down' is a grim reminder of pneumonic plague symptoms and the speed with which it killed.

THE GREAT COMPOSERS

Joseph Haydn

1732-1809

Joseph Haydn was one of the three great composers of the Viennese classical school, the others being Mozart and Beethoven. As can be seen from the development of his musical style, Haydn's lifetime saw the age of the Baroque give way to the Classical era; and as the inventor of the string quartet, 'Papa Haydn' is seen as one of the father figures of the Classical age. During his lifetime, Haydn's prestige was enormous: in 1809 when the French armies attacked and occupied Vienna, Napoleon ordered that a guard of honour should be placed at Haydn's door to protect the enfeebled composer from disturbance. Despite his great achievements, Haydn's reputation suffered after his death. This was partly a result of the change in musical style: the Romantic age rejected Haydn's cool Classicism in favour of the extreme and the unusual, and it is only in our own century that Haydn is again seen as the one of the greatest and most influential of composers.

Joseph Haydn spent much of his long life of nearly 80 years as Kapellmeister *to the Esterhazy family. It was at times an isolated existence, but as he himself wrote: 'There was no-one about me to confuse and torment me, and I was compelled to become original.' The following pages describe Haydn's life: his work for the Esterhazys, his unhappy marriage, his friendship with Mozart and his visit to London. Haydn's originality can be seen most clearly in his perfection of the early symphonic form, and* Listener's Guide *analyzes his achievements and examines in detail two of his greatest and best-known works – the 'Surprise' and the 'Clock' symphonies. Haydn's own life may have been relatively uneventful, but as* In the Background *describes, he witnessed the end of the ancien regime in Europe as it gave way to the convulsions of revolution and the imperial and military career of Napoleon Bonaparte.*

COMPOSER'S LIFE

'Papa Haydn'

Recognized in his lifetime as a composer of genius, Haydn, throughout his long musical career, was a central figure in the growth and development of the mature Classical style.

Regarded by his contemporaries as the father of modern instrumental music, Joseph Haydn was the first composer to recognize and develop the full potential of the evolving musical forms of the symphony and the sonata.

Born in 1732 he was the son of Mathias and Anna Maria Haydn. His father was a master wheelwright and a market magistrate (Marktrichter) and although an important man in the bureaucracy of the town of Rohrau – on the borders of Austria and Hungary – he was not well off. Joseph was the second of twelve children of whom only six survived infancy.

Neither of his parents had any musical training but his father loved folk songs and played the harp 'without knowing a note of music'. Joseph joined in the family's musical evenings and by the time he was five could sing many of his father's favourite songs with him – to the delight of family and friends who were all aware of this growing musical talent.

His first chance of advancement came when a relative, Johann Mathias Franck, visited the family in 1738. Franck was headmaster at the school in Hainburg and organist and director of music at the parish church of St Philip and St James. Hainburg itself was not much bigger than Rohrau, but it was decided that it would benefit Haydn to receive an education there. Although fascinated by the new sights and sounds around him the young Haydn did not have a very happy childhood in the Franck household, nor did he have an easy time at school under Franck's tutelage since Franck's preferred teaching method was to bash knowledge into the heads of his pupils.

Despite the unpleasant aspects of life in Hainburg Haydn did make musical progress. He learned to play every musical instrument and became a good singer. Although he never forgot the bad times in Hainburg he always regarded Franck's teaching as important. Long after he left Hainburg he recorded his debt to Franck:

I have to honour this man (Franck), even though he is long dead, for teaching me so many different things, even though I got more thrashings than food in the process.

When Haydn was seven, a second opportunity for

St Stephen's Cathedral, Vienna (right) where Haydn was a choirboy for eight years. He was recruited to the choir by Georg Reutter, the Kapellmeister at the Cathedral. Reutter had heard Haydn singing in the town of Hainburg where he received his early schooling.

A view of the Kohlmarket, Vienna (below), the area where Haydn lived after he was expelled from the cathedral choir in 1749. He rented a garret at the top of the Michaelerhaus, the large building on the right. In the left foreground are the premises of Artaria, who later became Haydn's publishers.

change in his musical education cropped up. He wrote in his autobiography:

When I was seven Kapellmeister von Reutter (of St Stephen's Cathedral in Vienna) passed through Hainburg and quite by accident heard my weak but pleasant voice. He forthwith took me to the choir house (of St Stephen's), where apart from my studies, I learned the art of singing, the harpsichord, and the violin, from very good masters. Until my eighteenth year I sang soprano with great success, not only at St Stephen's but also at Court. Finally I lost my voice.

When his voice changed he was no longer of any use to Reutter, who sought a pretext to dismiss him. When Haydn mischievously cut off the pigtail of a fellow-chorister Reutter expelled him.

Vienna is the city most associated with Haydn, but in fact, after his initial studies at St Stephen's Cathedral and his subsequent years of near starvation from 1749–1757, Haydn did not live in Vienna again until the last years of his life. When he was thrown out on the streets as a young boy of 18 he almost perished. Although he was lucky enough to meet and

Pietro Metastasio (above) an Italian poet, was one of the influential and successful literary and musical figures whom Haydn met when he was trying to earn his living in Vienna.

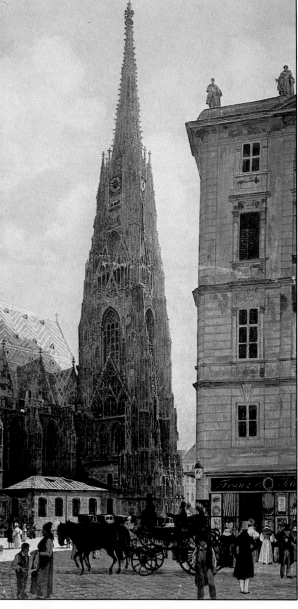

At first Haydn struggled as a freelance musician and teacher of music. Later, through his acquaintance with Metastasio and the composer Nicolo Porpora, his fortunes changed. Haydn was introduced to a world where he was able to make contact – at musical gatherings such as the one shown below, where he is represented playing the keyboard – with potential patrons.

share lodgings with Michael Spangler – an impoverished singer and music teacher – he led a very meagre existence. Gradually he made his way as a freelance musician – playing, teaching and composing diligently.

Through one of his pupils he met the Italian writer and poet Metastasio. At much the same time he met Nicolo Antonio Porpora, an Italian composer and became his valet and factotum. From Porpora he learned the true fundamentals of musical composition. As his assistant he had social access to the nobility – the only people in 18th-century society who could advance his career.

First court appointment

At one of the social and musical events to which Porpora introduced him he met an Austrian noble-man, Karl Joseph von Fürnberg. Von Fürnberg invited him to his country house in 1757 to take part in performances of chamber music. During this visit Haydn wrote his first string quartets, which were received with great enthusiasm. Von Fürnberg also recommended Haydn to Ferdinand Maximilian, Count von Morzin of Bohemia, who appointed Haydn his Kapellmeister in 1758. This was Haydn's first permanent musical post and he was paid 200 florins a year and received free board and lodgings. Haydn's duties were to organize all the music of the Count's orchestra of 16 musicians who played in Vienna during the winter and at his country estate in Lukaveč in the summer. Haydn's early quartets and symphonies dating from this period were very popular and were circulated in manuscript form throughout the Austrian Empire. His First Symphony was written for and performed by Count von Morzin's orchestra in 1759 – one of the guests at the performance was Prince Paul Anton Esterhazy – a wealthy nobleman who was to be Haydn's future employer.

An unsuccessful marriage

With some financial security behind him Haydn's thoughts turned to marriage. He had fallen in love with one of his pupils, Therese Keller, the daughter of a wig-maker in Vienna. It is thought that she did not return his affection and in 1756 she entered the convent of St Nicholas in Vienna. Haydn wrote this first major work, *Salve Regina in E major* for her induction. Whether he felt under an obligation to the family or was put under some pressure by them is not known, but in November 1760 he married Therese's older sister, Maria Anna. The marriage was not a success. It soon became evident that Maria Anna was ill-natured, indifferent to music and unsuited to domestic or family life.

According to reports from musicians who worked for Haydn she was always doing things designed to irritate him. They said that she used his manuscripts as lining paper for her pastry tins and paper for hair curlers. Whatever the truth of the matter she devoted much of her time to the church and Haydn turned to his music as an escape. Haydn enjoyed the company of women and given the unsuccessful nature of the marriage found companionship with a number of other women. Of his many women friends the most celebrated were the singer Luigia Polzelli (engaged to sing at Esterhazy in 1779) and Maria Anna von Genzinger, wife of one of the Esterhazy doctors.

Due to financial difficulties Count Morzin was forced to disband his orchestra in 1761 and Haydn

Archiv für Kunst und Geschichte

B. G. Pesci 'Esterháza' National Museum Budapest/Malvisi Archive

had to look for another post. Hearing that Haydn was unemployed, Prince Paul Anton Esterhazy offered him the post of Assistant Kapellmeister. One of the most powerful and wealthy Austro-Hungarian families, the Esterhazy family spent the summers at their palace in Eisenstadt and the winters in Vienna. Haydn was in charge of a small but brilliant orchestra and, on condition of giving satisfaction, was promised the post of Kapellmeister on the retirement or death of the incumbent, Werner.

For the next thirty years Haydn was involved at the court of the Esterhazys. In 1762 Prince Paul Anton died and was succeeded by his brother Prince Nikolaus, an extremely cultured man, who continued his brother's efforts to expand and modernize the Esterhazy musical repertoire. Haydn remained in his service until Nikolaus died in 1790. During this time Haydn wrote in every musical genre, both vocal and instrumental, and gained a reputation that made him the most famous composer in Europe.

Kapellmeister at Eszterhaza

The year 1766 was a turning point in Haydn's musical development. Werner, the Kapellmeister, died and Haydn was appointed to the post. This meant that he had total responsibility for all musical performances at court and was again able to compose church music (formerly this had been Werner's preserve).

Also in 1766 Prince Nikolaus moved the court to a palace which he had built on one of the family estates in Hungary at a place called Süttör. The palace, from 1765 known as Eszterhaza, was said to rival Versailles in beauty and splendour.

Two of the new facilities at Eszterhaza were a marionette theatre and an opera house. For both of these venues Haydn created successful and original works, but for the opera house he also rehearsed and performed works by other composers. Most of his own operas were written to celebrate special occasions like marriages, royal visits and name days.

At Eszterhaza Haydn was isolated from his musician friends in Vienna. The palace itself was remote and only visited by those invited by the Prince. Haydn, however, realized that the isolation was ultimately beneficial to him.

The theatre at Eszterhaza was opened in 1768, and as the Prince's interest in opera increased, the opera season was greatly extended. In 1786 there were 125 performances and 17 operas were staged.

In 1779 the opera house together with the collection of music which was housed in it, was destroyed by fire. Fortunately, Haydn kept the autographed scores separate from the performance material so the music was not lost. A more magnificent theatre was rebuilt in 1781 but Haydn wrote only three more operas for Eszterhaza.

Also in 1779 Haydn established a firm contact with the Viennese publishers, Artaria. Up until this time only one of Haydn's works had been published with his permission. Editions of his work which had appeared in other countries were probably published without his permission or even without his knowledge. In any case, prior to 1779 Haydn's compositions were really the property of Prince Nikolaus. Now, due to the terms of a new contract between himself and the Prince, Haydn was free to supply publishers with his work, and from 1780–1790 he entrusted most of his principal compositions to Artaria. Both he and the publishers made a good deal of money from the transactions and his reputation abroad grew at an astounding pace.

Haydn's relationship with the young singer Luigia Polzelli blossomed in 1779 when, together with her violinist husband, she was engaged at Eszterhaza. Luigia's marriage, like that of Haydn, was not a happy one and Haydn seemed to lavish on Luigia the affection he had not felt for his wife. Although Luigia seemed to have a sincere affection for Haydn, she was quick to see the benefit that the Kapellmeister's affection might have for her. When the orchestra was disbanded in 1790 Haydn and Luigia continued their friendship by letter. When Haydn's wife died in 1802

Prince Nikolaus Esterhazy (above left) succeeded his brother, Prince Paul Anton – Haydn's first Esterházy employer – in 1762. Prince Nikolaus was Haydn's patron and employer for nearly 30 years until his death in 1790. He was a cultured and artistic man who never grudged any money spent on splendid occasions. Before he succeeded to the title he spent much of his time at a hunting lodge which he had inherited at Süttör. He used it as a summer residence but enjoyed being there so much that he decided to rebuild it as a palace. From 1765 it was known as Eszterhaza and from 1766, the new palace (above) became his main court. It was here at Eszterháza that Haydn's musical activities were centred.

he signed a declaration that if he remarried it would only be to Luigia. However, Luigia returned to Italy when her husband died and shortly before Haydn's death married an Italian singer. It was rumoured that her second son, Antonio, born at Eszterhaza in 1783 was Haydn's illegitimate son.

In 1785 Haydn was accepted as a member of a Viennese lodge of Freemasons and probably through this contact (Mozart, too, was a Freemason) his friendship with Mozart grew. At a private evening concert in Vienna Mozart played three of the set of six new quartets which he dedicated to Haydn. After the performance Haydn told Mozart's father, Leopold, that he thought Mozart was the greatest composer he knew.

Haydn's last important works written at Eszterhaza were the Twelve Quartets, Op. 54, 55 and 64, written for Johann Tost, a violinist in the Eszterhaza orchestra. In 1790, Princess Elizabeth Esterhazy died in February and her husband, Haydn's patron, died seven months later. He was succeeded by his son, Anton, whose interests were more political than artistic and who had no interest in music. He disbanded the orchestra and the choir and though Haydn was retained, he remained as choir master in name only. He received a handsome pension from the estate of Prince Nikolaus but as there was nothing to keep him in Eszterhaza, he was free to travel and he decided to return to Vienna.

In Vienna he received an offer of employment from the King of Naples but, glad to have his independence once more, he was reluctant to take up the offer of a court post. A visit from Johann Peter Salomon, a German born violinist and London concert promotor, gave him another option. Salomon engaged him for a series of concerts in London.

The London visits

Haydn took leave of his friend Mozart at a farewell luncheon during which they both wept and Mozart was filled with a premonition that they would not see each other again – a feeling which sadly proved true. Haydn, who had travelled very little indeed and had never even seen the sea, set off with Salomon for England on 15 December 1790.

Under his contract with Salomon Haydn agreed to travel to London to conduct twenty concerts, each one to include a first performance of one of his own compositions. He would receive £300 for a new opera, £300 for six new symphonies as well as a further £200 for they copyright, £200 for his participation in the 20 concerts and a further £200 guaranteed for a benefit performance.

The first of the Salomon season of concerts took place on 11 March 1791, and it received a rapturous reception in the press and from the public. A rival

As court composer Haydn was required to produce church music, operas, symphonies and works for the baryton (the Prince's favourite musical instrument). Some of Haydn's operas were written and performed for name-day celebrations of members of his patron's family, or in celebration of special visits. L'incontro improvviso (below) was first performed in August 1775 when the Austrian Archduke Ferdinand and the Archduchess Beatrice, accompanied by the imperial court visited Eszterhaza.

Edward Dayes 'Hanover Square'/The Fotomas Index

Vigée-Lebrun 'Princes Marie Hermeneglid' Palais Liechtenstein/Malvisi Archive

concert organization known as the Professional Concerts had realized that a celebrity such as Haydn might win the entire London audience if there was no opposition. They promoted a series of concerts engaging another European musician, Ignaz Joseph Pleyel, who had been a pupil of Haydn's, as a counter-attraction. Both Haydn and Pleyel refused to take part in the rivalry which was being fostered and soon, after hearing both musicians, the London public was able to judge from performances which was the supreme genius of the two.

Haydn became a favourite of London society and many hoped that he would settle permanently in London. He was received by the Prince of Wales and was persuaded to stay in London for a second season. While in London, Oxford University conferred on him the title of Doctor of Music.

Haydn noted down everything which seemed quaint and unusual – London prices, English habits and customs, notes about people and music which he heard. He went to Ascot to watch the races and in November 1791 stayed with the Prince of Wales and his brother, the Duke of York, at Oatlands in Surrey. His closest friend in London was Rebecca Schroeter, widow of a German pianist and composer. She took piano lessons from Haydn and a strong friendship developed between them. Haydn kept her letters and in his old age showed them to a friend saying:

Those are from an English lady who fell in love with me. She was a very attractive woman, and still handsome, though over sixty; and had I been free I should certainly have married her.

At the beginning of 1792 Haydn heard the sad news of the death of his friend Mozart, aged 35. Later that year Haydn left London to return to Vienna. En route he stopped at Bad Godesburg where a young court composer submitted a cantata to him for his assessment. Haydn praised the cantata and promised to be the composer's teacher if he ever came to Vienna. The young composer was Beethoven and he took up the offer later that year when he came to Vienna. There were difficult moments in their relationship – Haydn once remarked, 'You give me the impression of being a man who has several heads, several hearts and several souls.'

Haydn was greatly affected in 1793 by the death of

The Hanover Square rooms, in the left background (above) saw Haydn's London's success.

Gesellschaft der Musikfreunde, Vienna.

Haydn's most important duty for his third Esterhazy patron, Prince Nikolaus II, was the composition every year of a new mass to celebrate the name-day of the Prince's wife, Princess Maria Hermenegild (left).

The crowning achievement of Haydn's old age was his oratorio, The Creation, *first performed in public in 1799. On 27 March 1808 a special performance (below) was given in the hall of the Old University in Vienna, to mark Haydn's 76th birthday. Haydn by this time was very frail and was carried into the hall from his coach.*

The last few weeks of Haydn's life were disturbed by the French bombardment of the suburbs of Vienna.

his great friend Maria Anna von Genzinger. He found life in Vienna was not as stimulating as the cultural life he had experienced in England, so in 1794 he set off again for London. This time he took with him his servant and copyist, Johann Elssler. His second London visit was even more successful than the first.

Haydn was introduced at Court and the King, George III, asked him to stay in England – the Queen even offered him a suite in Windsor Castle. Haydn gave the proposition serious thought but felt that he wanted to spend his remaining years in his home country. He was also probably alarmed by the increasing violence of the Napoleonic War, threatening to isolate England from the Continent.

The mature years in Vienna

However, in Austria his patron Prince Anton Esterhazy had died and his successor, Prince Nikolaus II requested Haydn to return as he had decided to reconstitute the princely band and choir. In August 1795 Haydn bade farewell to his many English friends and returned to Vienna. In England his art had expanded greatly and it seemed that not only was he inexhaustible but that his inspiration was unlimited. London broadened his horizons and he returned to Vienna a thoroughly sophisticated 18th-century gentleman.

In between his two London visits Haydn had purchased a house in a suburb of Vienna called Gumpendorf and it was to this house, newly enlarged in 1793, that he returned in 1795. His patron had abandoned Eszterhaza and established his summer residence at Eisenstadt. Haydn's duties, apart from the normal admistrative duties of Kapellmeister, were to produce a mass once every year for the name-day of Prince Nikolaus II's wife, Princess Maria Hermenegild. The series of six masses he wrote in celebration of his patroness, of whom he was particularly fond, are proof of his astonishing creativity. However the crowning achievement of

Haydn's old age was his oratorio, *The Creation*. He spent the whole of 1797 and part of 1798 working on this composition. His librettist Gottfried van Swieten organized a group of Viennese aristocrats who agreed to sponsor a private performance, each guaranteeing Haydn a sum of 500 ducats. This took place at the Schwarzenberg Palace on 29 and 30 April 1798. The work was so successful it had to be repeated on 7th and 10th May. After revisions the work had its first public performance at the Burg Theatre on 19 March 1799. Haydn conducted it and Salieri, the Emperor's Kapellmeister, played the pianoforte. The atmosphere was electric and the work was a resounding success.

Probably fired by the great success of *The Creation* Haydn and von Swieten decided to collaborate again on another oratorio. The text chosen was a poem by James Thomson, *The Seasons*. Haydn worked on the first part of *The Seasons* in 1799 but ill health hindered his progress and he left the last sections until 1801. The first performance was sponsored in the same way as *The Creation* and the first public performance took place at the Redoutensaal.

His unhappy marriage came to an end in 1802 when his wife died, but it was too late for him to think of remarriage. At this time, he began to put his affairs in order and in 1805 with Elssler drew up a thematic catalogue, the *Entwurf-Katalog*.

Although he had no close female companion in his old age, his patroness, Princess Maria Hermenegild, saw that he was comfortable and Prince Nikolaus's doctors attended him as he became more frail and ill. In the days preceding his death the French attacked Vienna and during one of the bombardments a cannon ball fell near the house. When the French took and occupied Vienna Napoleon placed a guard of honour at Haydn's door. Haydn died on 31 May 1809 of old age and exhaustion. He was buried in the cemetery at the Hundsturmer Linie but his body was reburied in 1820 by Prince Nikolaus at Eisenstadt.

LISTENER'S GUIDE
'Surprise' and 'Clock' Symphonies

Both these symphonies display Haydn's originality and his particularly wry sense of humour – and both are full of surprises!

When Haydn came to London in 1791 he had been writing symphonies for some 35 years, most of that time working with one orchestra. This allowed him to experiment with instrumental combinations and special effects, and to evolve a highly satisfactory symphonic formula that served as a foundation for no less than 81 of his total of 108 symphonies: a fast opening movement; a slow movement often in variation form; a Minuet with a contrasting central Trio section; and a rapid finale. Increasingly, he added a slow section at the start of the first movement.

Haydn never permitted this formula to lead him into stereotyped music. He used it, rather, as a mould into which he would constantly pour new material, shaping it according to the inexhaustible fantasies of his imagination. The two symphonies in this recording come from his final group of 12, written for London (where they were called 'Overtures'). They represent not only Haydn's greatest achievement in the formula but also one of the twin peaks of 18th-century symphonic art, standing side by side with the last symphonies written by Mozart.

Symphony no. 94 in G ('Surprise')

The newspaper reviews from 24 March 1792, the day after the first performance of Symphony no. 94 in the Hanover Square Rooms, London, reveal that the work was a resounding critical success. They also reveal that the most striking feature of the entire symphony had been a single drum stroke:

The Second Movement was equal to the happiest of this great Master's conceptions. The surprise might not be unaptly likened to the situation of a beautiful Shepherdess who, lulled to slumber by the murmer of a distant Water-fall, starts alarmed by the unexpected firing of a fowling piece. (Oracle).

Subsequently, the work became widely known as 'The Surprise Symphony'. Correctly, it should be called 'The Symphony of Surprises', for that famous bang on the drum is one of the least of them!

Programme notes

First movement: Adagio-Vivace assai
The slow introduction begins with a song-like phrase for oboes and bassoons which is balanced by a soft string reply that fades away. The woodwind phrase is repeated, strengthened by flutes, and the strings enter again, this time expanding into a shadowy, mysterious theme on cellos and basses that leads through a crescendo to three loud notes and a sudden *diminuendo* (quietening).

But now all mystery is banished in music that literally bursts with unrestrained vitality, bouncing at great speed into a full orchestral statement, horns and trumpets propelling the music forward. There is a brief pause for breath before the main theme is off again with renewed vigour, a solo oboe tilting the brass rhythm upward at a jaunty angle. When the second theme arrives it does so hesitantly, a limping rhythm introducing a garrulous melody on violins, joined by flutes, that quickly gains

In Fragonard's light-hearted painting (left) a young beau creeps up to surprise his lover. It was no doubt with a similar sense of relish and anticipation, that Haydn (above) thought up the 'surprise' in his Symphony no. 94.

in strength and makes way for a surprise guest: a third theme of grace and charm that has the flutes and oboes cooing with delight. In Haydn's beautifully constructed plan the 'exposition' of these themes is terminated by a brief full-orchestral passage *(codetta)*, and is then repeated intact, a quiet hopping rhythm on violins forging the link back to the beginning of the Vivace assai.

The development section begins uncertainly by taking a segment of the main theme and bending it up and down as if to test its resilience. Offended at this abuse, the music turns abruptly to anger, changing key in a storm of protest. The second theme adds its garrulous voice for a moment, and the fury seems in danger of getting out of hand. But in an instant the storm is over: the main theme returns smiling as the oboe's up-tilted rhythm abets the surprising new mood. We are already in the recapitulation, that part of a sonata-form movement in which melodies heard earlier are modified and restated.

Second movement: Andante
The second movement opens with a quiet, innocent theme of childlike simplicity. English-speaking children sing this theme, or its close relative, to *Twinkle, twinkle, little star*.

Example 1

At the end of the pianissimo second statement comes the 'Surprise' – a sudden fortissimo chord for the whole orchestra, underpinned by a loud drum stroke which, Haydn thought, would make all the ladies scream! There immediately follows the second half of the melody, played by strings and repeated with woodwind embellishments.

Haydn's original score did not include this famous 'Surprise' – he rewrote the opening of the Andante to appeal to the tastes of the sensation-loving London audience, then considered the most sophisticated audience in Europe. The 'Surprise' had its desired effect. As Haydn himself relates, '. . . the first Allegro of my Symphony had already met with countless Bravos, but the enthusiasm reached its peak at the Andante with the Drum Stroke. Encore! Encore! sounded in every throat...'

Now the orchestra, as Sir Donald Tovey entertainingly puts it, 'waddles through the poultry-yard in several variations . . .' and at one point, 'the oboe seems to have laid an egg'! The first variation maintains the childlike simplicity, violins and flute adding a graceful comment, as if moved to dance to the steady rhythm. Variation 2 commences sternly in C minor, the second half showing surprising strength and energy. But the music pauses, and violins take us gently into Variation 3. Now, each note is doubled by solo oboe, a procedure that clearly delights the flute, which joins the oboe in a heavenly duet. As this draws to a close the horns' gruff voices warn quietly of trouble ahead. It arrives (Variation 4) with a melody on brass and woodwind.

With breathtaking suddenness, Haydn switches mood yet again with a passage marked *pianissimo e dolce* (very quietly and sweetly). This is the biggest surprise so far, for we are now in the midst of Variation 5, for which Variation 4 has stood aside with a politeness quite out of character. At the end of this sweet episode the music hesitates, whereupon Variation 4 comes lumbering back, blowing itself out with fearsome brass and drum fanfares (Haydn was considered a noisy composer by his contemporaries). A delicate, apologetic coda draws a veil over the scene.

Third movement: Menuet and Trio: Allegro molto

Textbooks describe Minuet (*Menuet* in the French spelling Haydn often adopted) as a stately or graceful dance in moderate or slow tempo. By giving the present example the surprising tempo direction *Allegro molto* (very fast), Haydn was not only flouting convention but also looking forward to the type of minuet Beethoven was to call *Scherzo* ('a joke'). This lively minuet occupies an intermediate stage: too rapid in its swaying motion to be called 'stately' or 'moderate', yet not quite approaching the headlong pace of a fully-fledged Scherzo. Its form is conventional, however: two sections, each repeated, then a central Trio also in two repeated sections.

The Trio contains a curiously acrobatic melody on violins and bassoon, which is extended in the second part but does not stray far from the matter in hand. The expected repeat of the Minuet rounds off the movement.

Fourth movement: Allegro di molto

Haydn invented the form of this finale, which lies somewhere between sonata form and rondo. As in a rondo, the first theme occurs repeatedly, but here each appearance leads into unexpected developments. On its first appearance the theme is announced by violins, to which a flute is added in the repeat. Then comes a subsidiary idea which leads back to the first theme (bassoon joining flute and violins) bringing the first entry of the full orchestra. This is lightly scored, short notes and melodic fragments serving as background to a kind of perpetual motion in violins. It prepares for the second subject, which appears in a new key (D major). Pizzicato bass strings and a syncopated figure accompany this joyful second subject, but are soon swept aside by the *perpetuum mobile*. Three decisive chords close this episode.

Now a surprise interruption from wood-

Thomas Malton 'St. George's Hanover Square' The Museum of London

wind, brass and timpani diverts the music from its course into a passage of great excitement that could be regarded as the development section. Yet another appearance of the first theme features the return of the flute but it is soon interrupted by further development, starting in G minor and running through a series of keys until the violins are left bewildered, spinning frantically. They slip almost accidentally into the recapitulation: the flute is again present (together with bassoon), and the melody continues without interruption long enough for the flute to make a brief solo celebration of its return.

Another exciting episode leads to a repeat of the second theme and then to a series of imaginatively scored fragments of melody under which a forgotten voice mutters indignantly about neglect. Suddenly, with stunning impact, that voice, the drum, leaps out from the texture in a ferocious attack, far more disconcerting in the context of this high-spirited finale than had been that lone chord in the second movement.

After this, loose ends are tied in a virtuoso coda, woodwind supplying two impertinent penultimate chords.

Symphony no. 101 in D ('The Clock')

If anything, Haydn's second visit to London, after an 18-month 'holiday' at home in Vienna, was even more successful than the first. A new symphony, nicknamed 'The Clock', by 'the inexhaustible, the wonderful, the sublime HAYDN,' was greeted with open-mouthed admiration. 'It was HAYDN; what can we, what need we say more?' (Morning Chronicle).

George Romney 'The Gower Family' Christie's, London/Bridgeman Art Library

The 'Surprise' Symphony was first performed on 24 March 1792 in the Hanover Square Rooms on the east side of Hanover Street (left). It was a resounding critical success.

The famous second movement of the symphony is characterized by a childlike simplicity – echoed in the painting below; its innocent theme is sung by children to the words 'Twinkle twinkle little star'. After its second statement, when Haydn's audience would least expect it, comes a sudden, loud drumstroke – the notorious 'surprise' of the symphony.

The Symphony's nickname derives from the humorous rhythmic ticking figure that persists throughout the second movement, forming an insistent accompaniment.

Programme notes

First movement: Adagio. Presto

The solemn, quiet introduction seems to form itself out of a Thames fog, as indefinite, misty sonorities give rise to a slow-moving melody that feels its way uncertainly in the gloom. Suddenly the mists clear and the sun beams out as the Presto enters, springing upwards with great energy on first violins. It gathers in the rest of the orchestra and the music gambols joyfully for a space, flutes joining violins on the second presentation of the main theme. Now comes the traditional second subject, again clearly related to the main theme.

Example 2

Thomas Gainsborough 'Giovanna Baccelli'. The Tate Gallery, London

For the moment the music's happiness approaches hysteria, but the downward scale, first on violins, then on cellos and basses, cools the fever and returns the music to the beginning of the Presto section. This exposition repeat gives the listener the opportunity to notice that Haydn's phrases fall into unexpectedly irregular bar-groupings, which give the music a constant feeling of unpredict-ability. In fact, the only predictable thing about Haydn is that one can always rely on him to produce the unexpected!

This is illustrated in the development section. It starts with wispy references to Example 2 that gradually coalesce and grow menacing, the downward scale plunging the music into a turmoil of intense development, undertaken at breathtaking speed. By the middle of the development this carefree music has evolved into a stressful episode of warring themes that collide violently, the tension released at last on eight detached chords. Strings climb laboriously upwards, but the bright voice of a flute brings a welcome note of

The third movement is a cheerful Menuet and Trio – a fleet-footed dance (above) which Haydn takes at a more lively pace than was conventional.

gaiety and the development ends with the downward scale, as if nothing serious had happened at all.

Now comes the recapitulation, bringing surprises of its own. It is remarkably free, containing one of the biggest climaxes in the whole movement. Example 2 is transferred to cellos, who toss it boisterously to violins and catch it back again, and the intense anxiety of the development is soon glimpsed again, but now in full, glorious sunlight. As a final gesture of happiness the solo flute takes the main theme, and the end of the movement is like a hearty slap on the back.

Second movement: Andante

The 'clock' starts ticking immediately on two bassoons supported by pizzicato second violins, cellos and basses. This simple accompaniment, which becomes complicated later, serves to underlie a somewhat convoluted main theme:

Example 3

The whole movement revolves around this theme and its derivatives.

At the end of the first short section (marked by an upward-prancing bassoon figure) the theme is repeated (the bassoon prancing down again) and the second section begins with a derivative of C from Example 3. The music slides into D major to prepare for a second subject but Haydn merely takes a fragment from the first theme (A from Example 3), inverts it, squeezes the intervals together, and makes the result serve as a new idea, insolently tacking on B after the first four statements. A solo oboe holds a single note over those statements, then joins the violins for a repeat of the whole main theme, now

The 'Clock' Symphony opens quietly and uncertainly, until the Presto enters like sunlight breaking through mist (above).

substantially altered. The downward-prancing bassoon marks the end of this section.

Before it can complete this second statement the music is plunged into G minor and a new theme appears, the clock rhythm being maintained throughout by lower strings and woodwind. Soon, storm clouds gather around repeated nervous statements of the opening dotted rhythm (C from Example 3). As suddenly as it

Understanding music: Haydn and the symphony

The first composer to realize the potential of the symphonic form and exploit it to the full was Haydn. During his 30 years in the service of the Esterhazy family, Haydn was often musically isolated. He was forced to be original and inventive simply because there was nobody else to consult or copy. He had at his command a group of accomplished musicians and was given a free hand, more or less, to do exactly what he wanted.

Haydn enlarged the orchestra and proceeded to experiment tirelessly, producing an unending stream of matchless symphonies, in addition to a prodigious amount of other compositions. He is officially credited with over 100 numbered symphonies but, confusingly, they are not numbered chronologically. All have been recorded at least once on disc, and this enormous, well documented output enables us to trace his developing mastery of the medium.

In 1761, when Haydn was just 29, he produced his first symphonies (nos. 6, 7 and 8) for the new Esterhazy orchestra. They formed a trilogy, and were labelled by the composer *Le Matin, Le Midi,* and *Le Soir* (Morning, Noon and Evening). These three early compositions were scored rather like the old Baroque concertos, with scattered solo instrumental passages.

Among the musicians at Haydn's disposal were four gifted horn players. It was no doubt with them in mind that he composed his Symphony no. 31 (the 'Hornsignal') in 1765. It is a hunting symphony, noted for its extremely difficult horn passages. A famous composition from Haydn's middle period is

Symphony no. 55, nicknamed the 'Schoolmaster' (above), sparkles with Haydn's sophisticated wit.

Symphony no. 45 (the 'Farewell'), written in the unusual key of F sharp minor. The Symphony derives its nickname from the moment in the last movement when the performers stop playing one by one, snuff out their candles, and leave the platform in turn until finally only two violinists remain. It was Haydn's wry way of hinting that they were all ready for a holiday.

There followed a tense emotional interlude for Haydn, which has been referred to as his *Sturm und Drang* period. This is a German phrase meaning 'storm and stress' and describes a German literary movement of the late 1700s that was characterized by high emotionalism and which marked the first stirrings of Romanticism. Eight symphonies in particular clearly highlight this period of Haydn's life, Symphony no. 49 *(La Passione)* through to Symphony no. 56 and the use of minor keys.

By the 1780s Haydn had become internationally famous. At that time he was commissioned to write a set of six symphonies for a Parisian music society. These became known as the Paris Symphonies and carry distinctive nicknames such as no. 82, *L'Ours* (The Bear), no. 83, *La Poule* (The Hen), and no. 85, *La Reine* (The Queen).

In 1790 Haydn, loaded with honours, was pensioned off and given a house in Vienna. Very soon he travelled to London, at the invitation of impresario Johann Salomon. It was the first of two successful and rewarding visits, and while there, Haydn composed two sets of six symphonies each, collectively known as the London or Salomon Symphonies. Among them is the 'Surprise' (no. 94), with its sudden loud chord intended to awaken sleepy listeners; the 'Clock' (no. 101), with its humorous tick-tock movement; the 'Drum Roll' (no. 103); and the 'Miracle' (no. 96). The last-named earned its nickname from an incident which, in fact, occurred during the performance of Symphony no. 102; a chandelier crashed down on the audience injuring nobody – a 'miracle' – and the nickname was mistakenly assigned to no. 96.

These London symphonies represent the peak of Haydn's symphonic achievement. They delight and stimulate the ear with striking effects – unexpected modulations, sudden crescendos, changes of rhythm, flashes of humour. They reveal the composer as a good-natured, unpredictable genius who developed the artistic freedom to express a wide range of emotions within a coherent musical idea.

F. Bergamini 'Village School'/Archiv für Kunst und Geschichte

*Like the 'Surprise' Symphony, this work
derives its nickname from a humorous
effect in the slow movement – an insistent
rhythm on bassoons and strings which
sounds like the ticking of a clock (above).
At one point the clock stops – and then
starts up again.*

arrives, however, the storm abates, leaving
the clock ticking comically on flute and
bassoon duet, while violins placidly repeat
the main theme.

Then – abruptly – the clock stops!

When it resumes, the key has changed
(to E flat), and the ticking is carried
by second violins. First violins try
unsuccessfully to restart the main theme,
to the annoyance of an irrascible flute, and
the orchestra flares irritably for a moment,
then marks time as if considering how best
to continue. The main theme bursts in, in
the original key, horns strengthening the
tick-tock accompaniment, and a busy
violin figuration sweeps the music along.
At the first sign of flagging, horns again
support the rhythm and the final statement
of the theme is forcefully given out by full
orchestra, including drums and trumpets.

Third movement: Menuet and Trio: Allegretto
The outer sections of this movement, the
Menuet itself, are in the same overall plan
as the Menuet in the 'Surprise' Symphony,
but in other respects the two movements
could hardly be more dissimilar. Whereas
the Menuet in the 'Surprise' Symphony was
fleet-footed, light and cheerful, the present

*The third movement is a stately Minuet.
Its measured pace suggests an elegant
couple promenading (right).*

one is triumphant, measured, and highly-developed. The first section sets the stately mood with sonorous scoring and firm rhythm. The second part opens quietly on violins while drum insists softly on the rhythm. A brief interchange between oboes, bassoons and horns leads to a short contrasting section that brings a modified version of the first section.

'We have never heard a more charming effect than was produced by the Trio to the Minuet,' wrote the *Morning Chronicle* critic in his review. It is indeed a charming idea, incorporating one of Haydn's sly jokes. Strings commence a drone-like accompaniment, but for a moment the listener is led to believe that the soloist has forgotten to enter. At last, a flute produces a simple melody, on the top four notes of which the strings should change their harmony, but they omit to do so, resulting in a clash between F and E. Today's ears are accustomed to such mild discords but in Haydn's day the clash would have startled his listeners, so, for the repeat, violins make the adjustment and all is well.

Fourth movement: Vivace

The rising phrases heard earlier in the Symphony find an echo in the main theme of the finale: three long rising notes, a downward rush, then four short rising notes, the whole rounded off with a balancing phrase. This is repeated. Contrasting material brings a restatement, then this section, too, is repeated.

That downward rush launches the next section, as the music bursts into a whirlwind of excitement. At length a solo oboe is left hopping on one foot before joining the first violins in a syncopated passage that brings yet more exhilarating writing: the orchestra pounds out the three long notes while violins and flute maintain constant running momentum. The 'second subject', following a single detached chord, is in reality only a modification of the first, into which it quickly slides.

With startling abruptness, the music drops into D minor for a long, fierce passage, driven relentlessly by brass fanfares. A change back to D major brings what promises to be a quiet recapitulation. This, however, declares itself to be nothing less than a huge fugue, the first theme scurrying about among the various strings in a bewildering display of virtuoso composition. Soon, oboes, bassoons and horns enter with the three long notes, and as these gain supremacy the symphony is brought to a breathless conclusion.

Reviews of the 'Clock' Symphony (above) were even more enthusiastic than those that greeted the 'Surprise': 'Every new Overture [Symphony] he writes, we fear, till it is heard, he can only repeat himself; and we are every time mistaken.'

Great interpreters

London Philharmonic Orchestra

The London Philharmonic Orchestra (LPO as it is commonly known), was formed by Sir Thomas Beecham in 1932 after he had failed to come to terms with any of the existing orchestras in London. He decided the only way to succeed was to have his own orchestra. Under his guidance, the LPO quickly proved its mettle and became the leading London orchestra up to the beginning of World War II. During this period, the LPO gave its own concerts, performing for the Royal Philharmonic Society and giving summer international opera seasons at Covent Garden. In 1936 it completed a famous tour of Germany along with Beecham.

Sir Thomas left England for the USA at the outbreak of war, but instead of disbanding, the orchestra formed a management committee of its own players and ran its own affairs. In this way the LPO remained active during the war and, when Beecham returned in 1945, they decided not to re-engage him as director. Thus they remained a self-governing body, relying on a steady stream of distinguished guest conductors. In 1949 the orchestra made its first permanent conducting appointment, and Eduard van Beinum became principal conductor. The same year, the London County Council gave the orchestra a grant of £25,000 per annum which gave the group a measure of financial and artistic security. However, that grant was discontinued in 1951, precipitating a long series of financial crises which were only eventually solved by the generosity of people both inside and outside the orchestra and through the termination of players' contracts in 1957 in favour of separate concert engagements for each individual player.

Sir Adrian Boult had succeeded Eduard van Beinum as principal conductor in 1951, and was particularly helpful during the orchestra's years of crisis. He was made honorary president in 1958. The rebuilding of finances and musical reputation continued under William Steinberg, 1958–62, John Pritchard, 1962–70 (Artistic Director 1967–70), and Bernhard Haitink, who was Artistic Director from 1970–79. Sir George Solti has split his time between Chicago and the LPO since 1979.

The orchestra's history-making tour of the USSR in 1956 (the first by a British orchestra) and their 1970 tour of the USA had broadened its reputation among musicians and general audiences alike, while its regular presence at Glyndebourne (near the south coast of England) since 1964 has also stood it in good stead. Today the LPO is highly-esteemed and still self-governing after all these years.

FURTHER LISTENING

Haydn

Cello Concerto in D (1783)
Haydn was never an instrumental virtuoso; this fact, plus a lack of commissioning opportunities, kept his concerto writing to a minimum. None of the surviving concertos are essential to his great achievement as a composer, but that hardly detracts from the pleasure to be derived from this work. The solo part holds little in the way of technical terrors for the seasoned player, but the work as a whole is beautifully proportioned and has the sweetness and dignity which is so characteristic of Haydn's better work.

String Quartet, op. 76 nos. 1–6 (1799)
Haydn composed for the string quartet for the greater part of his creative life, and was influential in determining the form's very nature. The six quartets which go to make up opus 76 are works of Haydn's maturity, and radiate warmth and sincerity. Each quartet reveals a different side of the composer's creative nature, just as each also solves a particular musical problem. No. 2 in D Minor has the famous 'Witches' Minuet', a strange exercise in octave doubling, while the Sixth Quartet contains moments of astonishing beauty and repose.

The Creation – Oratorio (1798)
The Creation, whose libretto was modelled on Milton's *Paradise Lost* – translated into German, translated back again into English, rejected by other composers and finally set to music by Haydn – is a triumph of musical wit and imagination. Despite the second-rate libretto, Haydn's music is conceived with the utmost dignity, and coloured by a deep humility and humanity. The work is recognized as a true masterpiece of the genre.

IN THE BACKGROUND
'Vive la Nation'

When the French people rose against their king, Louis XVI, in 1789 the shock waves caused by the forces of revolution were felt in almost every country in Europe.

Carnavalet/Bulloz

At about half past ten at night, on 20 June 1791, King Louis XVI and Queen Marie Antoinette of France, together with their two children, the King's sister Madame Elizabeth, and the royal governess, slipped out of the Tuileries Palace by an unwatched door and into a waiting carriage. The King was wearing the clothes of a valet; the Queen was dressed to look like a governess; and the six-year-old dauphin was dressed up as a little girl. The governess, for the moment alias 'Baroness Korff', appeared as the employer of these royal servants and mother of the boy and girl, and the coachman was none other than Count Fersen, a handsome young Swede who was devoted to the Queen and who had been involved in drawing up the escape plan.

At the gates of Paris the getaway party changed into a heavier coach, prepared for a long journey, and at a slow pace took the road east. The little town of Varennes was reached between 11 and 12 on the night of 21 June. More than once in their slow progress the royal family had been recognized but allowed to pass on. Apart from the ineffectiveness of

their 'disguises' – the King's face was on every assignat, the new paper currency – the spanking new green and white coach, drawn by six horses, was also very conspicuous. That they had managed to reach Varennes was a matter of luck, given the Queen's insistence that the family travel together, for this decision prevented the use of a smaller, faster vehicle. It was the delays that were to prove fatal for the fugitives.

By stealing out of Paris this way the King was turning his back on the revolution that had started in 1789. He was heading eastwards to set up the royal standard at Metz, and to meet the Marquis de Bouille who was in command of an army with royalist sympathies. With the help of the other monarchs of Europe, particularly his brother-in-law, the Emperor Leopold of Austria, and the King of Prussia, Louis then hoped to defeat the revolutionaries and reconquer France for the *ancien régime* and to restore himself as an absolute monarch. However, these hopes were never to be fulfilled and Louis was destined to lose both his crown and his life.

On July 14th 1789 an armed mob, made up of Parisian craftsmen and shopkeepers, stormed the Bastille (far left). And despotisim, as symbolized by this great prison fortress was overthrown with the collapse of its defences – the Revolution had begun.

From the seclusion of his magnificent chateau in Versailles, Louis XVI (left) felt answerable only to God in the way he ruled his people. But his was a kingdom wracked with problems about which he was tragically ill-informed. It was a country divided by a rigid class system, weighed down by oppressive taxes and brimming over with the anger of the oppressed poor – ideal fuel for revolution.

The monarchy and the revolution

Unlike his predecessors Louis XIV (the Sun King) and Louis XV, Louis XVI was not an imperious autocrat, but he was very stubborn and woefully ill-informed. And from the seclusion of the royal chateau he had been blind to the true state of the nation and the plight of his people. When revolution came in 1789 Louis was not swept away; instead the revolutionary forces offered him a revised role – that of constitutional monarch who would reign by sanction of a national assembly of elected representatives. In a bid to cling to his throne, Louis at first went along with this, but in truth he did not see why he could not carry on as before – ruling alone by divine right rather than being merely the mouthpiece of an elected parliament. When finally the Assembly looked to re-structuring the clergy, Louis' will to continue with the new order broke.

He was intensely religious and he disliked the revolutionary idea that the property of the church belonged to all believers, not just the clergy, and that it was at the disposal of the nation. Still less did he like the new laws, enshrined in the Civil constitution of the Church which the Assembly passed in 1790, whereby bishops and priests were to be elected. By this new arrangement the lower clergy benefitted from a doubling of their incomes, to be paid by the state, and by the destruction of the old aristocratic monopoly on senior appointments such as bishoprics. Then a further decree, passed early in 1791, required all holders of clerical offices to take an oath of allegiance to the state, and the King's misgivings were confirmed and supported when the Pope condemned outright the whole Civil Constitution in March and April. From then on Louis' resolve to flee hardened.

In secret, he made moves towards armed intervention by his fellow monarchs and began his plans to escape in order to marshall counter-revolutionary forces.

Marie Antoinette

In less troubled times Louis had enjoyed nothing better than to retire to his workshop and forge, where he used to indulge in his favourite hobby of lockmaking, and he would come down to his wife's parties, and scoldings, with forge-blackened hands. Whereas Louis on the one hand was too mild and dull a character to manage a great historical crisis, his more assertive wife was dangerously susceptible to dramatic initiatives.

The story of Marie Antoinette's 'Let them eat cake' response to the plight of the bread-starved people of Paris has a very dubious basis in fact but, like many such stories, it does reflect a historical reality. Long before the revolution began Louis XVI's unhappy queen had acquired great unpopularity. Much of her bad image was very unfairly based on the fact that she was Austrian, the living symbol of an unpopular alliance through marriage between France and its traditional enemy, Austria. No sooner had she arrived at Versailles than the young Hapsburg princess had to run the gauntlet of various court factions who were hostile to the Austrian connection. But Marie Antoinette was not a conciliatory person, and she responded by withdrawing into a private little world and mingling only with her intimates.

Marie Antoinette was a pleasure-loving and extravagant queen and she made it too obvious when she was bored with some of her royal duties. Her

The French 'parliament' – for what it was worth – was divided into three estates: the aristocracy, the clergy and the middle-class professionals and businessmen who represented the masses. The Third Estate, as the latter group were known, fearing they could always be outvoted, demanded a large percentage of the votes. It was their political awakening (below) that spelled disaster for the King.

REVEIL DU TIERS ETAT.

dislike of stuffy court ceremonies was such that her mother, the Empress Maria Theresa, often tried to warn her about the consequences of such behaviour.

I know very well how tedious and futile is a representative position; but believe me, you will have to put up with both tediousness and futility, for otherwise you might suffer from much more serious inconveniences than these petty burdens – you more than most rulers, since you have to rule over so touchy a nation.

When the revolution happened Marie Antoinette was to realize just how touchy her subjects were. But she had no political sense and a disastrous habit of making enemies out of the people who could have helped her and her mild-mannered husband. Of the shrewd statesman Mirabeau she wrote disdainfully, 'We shall never be so wretched, I believe, as to be reduced to the painful extremity of having recourse to Mirabeau.' Yet his advice to the royal pair was sound. He told the King to accept the moderate revolutionary constitution, which did leave him with considerable powers such as the right to veto legislation, and to stand by the people and their parliamentary representatives as a constitutional king. Likewise advised General Lafayette, the liberal aristocrat who had fought for the Americans during their recent revolution. Lafayette also believed that there was a role for the King in the new France, if he

Carnavalet/Bulloz

The deputies of the Third Estate declared themselves to be the representative National Assembly and for solidarity took an oath (above left) which bound them to remain in session until their demands were met and they were joined by the other two Estates.

After their daring but ill-fated escape to Varennes, the King and his family were brought back to face the angry crowd of Paris (left). Their flight had destroyed once and for all, any possibility of retaining a constitutional monarchy.

In 1789, General Lafayette (below), presented a declaration of rights to the National Assembly. It was based on the American Declaration of Independence (he had taken a major part in the American war), but his struggle for order and humanity was in vain.

played his cards right, but he too was spurned. In April 1791 Mirabeau died, despairing of a monarchy that he believed was doomed. Then the Queen, ardently encouraged by her intimates, began to make plans, not for a compromise with democracy but for escape and revenge.

Disaster at Varennes

Just before the cumbersome coach reached Varennes its occupants had been recognized by a staunch young patriot.

In the coach there was a woman whom I thought I recognized as the Queen and on the seat in front of her to the left was a man. I was struck by the resemblance of his face to the likeness of the King printed on an assignat which I had with me at the time.

This was a posting master named Drouet (the posting station was the stage where carriages on long journeys changed postillions and horses) and he acted promptly on his hunch. Riding in pursuit, he learned of the coach's forward route and galloped across the countryside quickly enough to close the road. Varennes was actually within easy reach of Bouille's army and safety but, because of incompetence and bad luck, by the time the troops he had sent to meet the royal family arrived in the town the King had already been arrested and the fugitives were surrounded by bands of hostile peasants. Even then, Bouille's troops could have saved the day if they had challenged the King's captors because the revolutionaries' guns were not loaded. Drouet refused the substantial reward offered by the Assembly after Varennes but a year later he got himself elected as a deputy.

From Varennes the tragic return journey began. It took three and a half days because of the roundabout route adopted in order to avoid hostile crowds and all the while the royal coach needed the protection of National Guards and the presence of several deputies. Slowly, ignominiously and painfully the royal family arrived back at the palace that they loathed, surrounded as it was by the truculent citizens of Paris and cut off from the joys of hunting and the pleasures of the Petit Trianon. In the course

C. Bevilacqua/AISA

of this sad week the young Queen aged rapidly and it was said that her hair turned grey.

The counter-revolutionary menace

As yet it was only the King's status, not his life, that was endangered by the flight. So despite the fact that Louis had left behind a signed document repudiating all the measures he had accepted during his 'captivity' and despite the fact that royal fleurs-de-lis crests were being defaced in the streets, the Assembly still believed that the King was necessary and desirable as the head of state – they even put about the fiction that, far from having fled his people, the royal family had been 'abducted'. And although the King was temporarily disgraced by being suspended from his duties and rights, the new

The Paris crowd stormed the Tuileries (right), residence of the royal family, on August 10th 1792. Louis' Swiss Guard, ordered to cease fire by the King, were massacred.

The Marseillaise (below) was composed in 1792 by a French captain of engineers and amateur musician. It was sung by revolutionary troops marching to Paris from Marseilles – and was later named after the city.

constitution adopted in October 1791 duly installed him as the head of state.

Still Louis hoped that his court in exile, *France extérieure,* would deliver him as the escape fiasco had drawn international attention to his situation. Europe did seem to be resounding with denunciations of the revolution and little congregations of aristocratic émigrés, dedicated to a restoration of all their privileges and the King's former powers, were gathering around France's frontiers. Koblenz in Germany, where the King's brother, the Comte d'Artois, had installed himself, was full of such émigrés and they were confident of the military support of the outraged monarchs of Europe. The émigrés urged officers in the French army to desert their regiments and the women sent little dolls to titled gentlemen remaining in France as tokens of their contempt for anyone who compromised with the Revolution.

But the other European powers were in fact luke-warm as far as action against revolutionary France was concerned. They were more worried about what Catherine the Great was up to in Poland and some countries, like Britain, considered it quite useful that France's internal turmoil distracted her from military activity in the rest of Europe. But eventually Marie Antoinette's brother, Leopold of Austria, stirred himself. In August 1791, at Pilnitz, he and the King of Prussia undertook to avenge any offence against the French royal family and take joint action to restore order in France *if* the other powers would join them. But since there was no question of

Louis' final words – 'that he had wished for nothing but good for his people' – fell on deaf ears. Cheers of 'Vive la Nation' rose from the blood-crazed crowd as the King was executed and his severed head held up for all to see (right).

such a united front, this declaration was a hollow threat.

Attack on the Tuileries

Marie Antoinette saw through Leopold's cynical gesture immediately but the Pilnitz Declaration was seen by the people of France as an insult and an ultimatum. The country was gripped by a nightmare image of Austrian and Prussian armies, led by the émigrés and supported by traitors within, descending on them to crush the gains of the revolution. Some deputies began to argue that France should declare war first, attack being the best defence. Besides, the democratic refugees from neighbouring countries who thronged Paris, reassured the Assembly that their peoples would welcome the revolutionary armies – 'The French people will utter a great shout and every other nation will answer its call.' It was also hoped that the war effort would help to stabilize popular commitment to the revolution. In April 1792 the Assembly approved a declaration of war against Austria.

As the Austrian and Prussian armies mobilized tension mounted in France, particularly in the unruly capital city which had led the revolution. The King and Queen were in an impossible situation, for Louis was still the head of revolutionary France and the advancing enemies were his friends. So while Louis signed the decree that initiated the war, Marie Antoinette was secretly sending details of the French military plans over the border, and both King and Queen were praying for a counter revolutionary victory.

'La patrie en danger' (The country in danger) became the call throughout France as a state of emergency was declared, and those with faltering courage were roused by the sight of the men of Marseilles marching to their new patriotic song, the *Marseillaise.* But the royal family's situation grew more and more precarious as the fraught summer days passed. In one incident a mob swarmed into the palace and forced the King to don a cap of liberty and drink to the nation's health. The King handled this potentially ugly confrontation with great composure, but future crowds would be less easy to humour, less willing to trust him. Unfortunately, it was possibly the relative harmlessness of this crowd that disinclined the King to pay attention to Lafayette's new escape plan.

The Parisian crowd's mood was to change drastically with the Brunswick Manifesto of August 1792. The Duke of Brunswick was the commander of the counter-revolutionary allies and though his manifesto's contents derived from proposals first put forward by Louis and Marie Antoinette, he had allowed the émigrés to word it in the most provocative way possible. It ordered Paris to submit at once to the King upon pain of an 'exemplary and ever memorable vengeance' and the delivery of the city to 'military punishment and total destruction'. Once again the King had not been particularly well served by his friends for nothing could have been more calculated to identify the monarchy with the invader and concentrate anger against the throne.

On 10 August the Tuileries Palace was attacked by a huge and extremely hostile crowd. Recognizing the peril of their situation, the royal family fled for protection to the National Assembly. But in the ensuing riot in the Tuileries more than 1,000 people were killed – shot or trampled underfoot. The King was now stripped of all his remaining constitutional powers as anti-royalist feeling in Paris ran high. Many of the deputies in the Assembly sincerely believed that the Tuileries rising had saved Paris from an aristocratic plot designed to coincide with the counter-revolutionary invasion. But the rising meant

J. Bertaux 'Conquest of the Tuileries'. Versailles/AISA

Carnavalet/Bulloz

After a three-day trial, looking worn out and far older than her years, Louis' pleasure-loving and extravagant queen was sentenced to death. With her head shorn and wearing a simple white dress, Marie Antoinette rode to her place of execution in a cart.

David 'Marie-Antoinette'/Bulloz

Maximilien Robespierre (right), labelled the 'incorruptible', dominated the Committee of Public Safety during its brief period of power which included the Reign of Terror.

Bearing the symbols of the French worker, the poster shown far right carries the bold message of revolution – liberty, equality, fraternity or death!

J. M. Moreau 'Robespierre'. Versailles/Scala

UNITE. ET INDIVISIBILITE DE LA RÉPUBLIQUE. LIBERTÉ, ÉGALITÉ, FRATERNITÉ OU LA MORT

Carnavalet/Bulloz

the end of the constitutional monarchy, from now on France would be a republic. This meant that anyone who wished to restore the monarchy was a traitor, because they were also necessarily wishing for a national defeat at the hands of foreign powers and the émigrés.

The September massacres
By 2 September Verdun, only 140 miles from Paris, was taken by the invaders. The wildest rumours now circulated in the panic-stricken city. It was widely believed that when the invading forces were within reach of Paris, a 'fifth column' of priests and aristocrats would break out of the prisons to strike at peaceful citizens and murder the families of the men who had marched to the frontiers to defend *la patrie*. This was tinder for the appalling 'September Massacres', a series of gruesome incidents in which the inmates of Paris's prisons were slaughtered by historical crowds while the national security forces turned a blind eye.

The grisly September Massacres were the beginning of a phenomenon that was to evolve into the 'Reign of Terror'. It was not long now before the guillotine – so named after Dr Guillotin who had recommended it as a humane means of execution because of the speed with which its blade fell from a great height – would begin to rise and fall, and one of its first prominent victims was to be the King.

Execution of the King
Revolutionary confidence shot up with the first military victory at Valmy at the end of September, but this did not make the Assembly (now the Republican Convention) feel any more charitable towards the King. Since the attack on the Tuileries, the King had been redundant and, ever mindful of the temper of the uncomfortably close Parisian crowd, the deputies argued and debated about what was to be done with him. Did the abolition of the monarchy mean the elimination of the King, and if

not what should be done with him? Should he be impeached for crimes against the people, or was this even necessary if kingship itself were considered a crime? Finally, the deputies decided that some sort of trial was in order and the King, now confined in the grim tower of the Temple, was brought before them.

Standing at the bar, Louis denied that he had ever wished to shed the blood of his poeple but he never challenged the Convention's right to try him. His timid defence was then completely undermined when an iron chest containing royal private papers was found in the Tuileries. Here was the desperate correspondence between Louis (and Marie Antoinette) and foreign powers, between Louis and Mirabeau, and so on. Unmistakable evidence of his double dealing, there was no shadow of a doubt now as to the King's guilt. The Tuileries correspondence proved to be the King's and ultimately the Queen's, death warrant, for the deputies now voted by an overwhelming majority for his execution.

On the morning of 21 January 1793 'Louis Capet, last King of the French', was publicly executed. The guillotine was placed in the Place de la Revolution (now Place de la Concorde) and surrounded by soldiers and representatives of the local Paris assemblies. Louis was taken to the scaffold in the mayor's carriage, with the curtains drawn, and he bore himself with quiet dignity. He tried to make a final speech but his words were so drowned by the drums that it was impossible to catch what he said.

The Reign of Terror
Although the execution of the King provoked a great storm of outraged protest abroad – London went through a period of general mourning – in France itself there was surprisingly little reaction. The war was distracting and the fact that France was not threatened by virtually every power in Europe encouraged a desperate 'we'll show 'em' attitude. But despite the many achievements of the revolutionary armies, they were over-extended and a serious

reversal of fortunes had set in by March. At the same time, the Vendée, a region on the west coast, flared up in revolt against the revolution, particularly its religious legislation. The struggle against this rising and the renewed war effort brought with it more economic hardship, and to meet the crisis the Convention appointed a Committee of Public Safety in the summer of 1793. The men on this committee, notably Robespierre, did succeed in driving foreign armies from France, in crushing the royalist threat in the Vendée, stabilizing the economy and alleviating distress from hunger. But it achieved this at a great price in the form of the bloodiest phase in French history, the Reign of Terror.

The death of the Queen

The Terror, which lasted until the Committee was overthrown a year later, claimed the lives of an estimated 40,000 'enemies of the revolution' in the name of national security. And those who suffered first were the nobles who had not yet fled France, and who were now rounded up and thrown into the gloomy dungeons of the notorious Concièrgerie Prison. Here the widowed Queen herself was brought to await a three-day trial and in October 1793 Marie Antoinette was guillotined.

Louis' Queen was 38 years old when she died. After Marie Antoinette's execution Marie Grossholz, a talented young wax-modeller, was brought to the prison where the Queen's body had been carried in a handcart. There she was asked to make a death-mask of the features she had known in those far-off days of royal Versailles. Later, as that intrepid business-woman and survivor, Madame Tussaud, Marie made her waxworks into the basis of a 'chamber of horrors', which was to become a highly commercial and grisly memorial to the violent consequences of mass paranoia.

Marie Antoinette was soon followed to the scaffold by her pious sister-in-law, Madame Elizabeth, and in 1795 her young son, styled Louis XVII by his exiled subjects, died in captivity. The eight-year-old boy was said to have died of a kind of tuberculosis, and he had been a delicate child, but foul play was suspected. His sister, Marie-Thérèse, was more fortunate. After the overthrow of the Committee of Public Safety in July 1794 Austria managed to secure her release in exchange for some members of the Convention who were their prisoners. And by a strange twist of fate these prisoners included the Deputy Drouet, the quick-thinking posting master who had been responsible for the King's arrest on that dreadful night at Varennes.

Epilogue

With Robespierre and his followers gone – either deported or victims of the guillotine that had dispensed so effectively with thousands of their opponents – the terror finally ended. The coup that overthrew the Committee of Public Safety came as a result of mounting hostility towards Robspierre's independent authority and his puritancial vision of a 'Republic of Virtue'. The Committee itself had already been weakened by divisions in its ranks over the wars that were being waged in Europe.

These had been years of confusion and chaos, and in a bid for stability the Convention submitted a new constitution. They recommended that they should be replaced by a new legislative system, but retained the right of automatic re-election of two thirds of their members, and that their main rivals be disenfranchised.

The royalists, who had until then been hoping for a chance to restore the monarchy, rose in revolt to prevent the new constitution coming into effect. Royalists bourgeoisie and aristocrats converged on the Convention, but the rebellion was successfully crushed, the Convention and the republic saved by a young Corsican artillery officer who took charge. His name – Napoleon Bonaparte.

When in-fighting threatened to destroy the gains made by revolution and the establishment of the Republic, Napoleon (below) stepped in and took control by force. In defeating the foreign powers threatening France, Napoleon instilled confidence in the French people and in turn he was regarded as their saviour.

Philippoteaux 'Bonaparte at Rivoli'. Versailles/Edimedia

Contemporary composers

William Boyce (1711-79)

Born in London, Boyce was a choirboy at St. Paul's Cathedral, then in 1734 he became organist to the Earl of Oxford and composer to the Chapel Royal in 1736. Finally he was made Master of the King's Music in 1757, in which post he produced two odes each year. The overtures to these formed the basis of his *Twelve Overtures* of 1770 and two others were included in his *Eight Symphonies* of 1760, where Handel's influence is apparent. Increasing deafness later forced him to retire and concentrate on compiling his *Cathedral Music,* whose three volumes covered some 200 years of English church music. After his death in 1779, Boyce was buried in St. Paul's Cathedral, London.

Dietrich Buxtehude (1637-1707)

Born in Oldesloe, north Germany, Buxtehude became organist at the German church in Elsinore, Denmark before taking up the post of organist at Lübeck cathedral that he occupied for the rest of his life. There he continued the series of *Abendmusiken* (Sunday evening concerts), which came to comprise a mixture of sacred vocal music (oratorios and cantatas), organ recitals and chamber concerts. Such was Buxtehude's fame as an organist that the young Bach travelled 200 miles on foot to hear him play in 1705. Buxtehude wrote about 120 sacred vocal pieces, of which *Jesu meine Freude* is probably the best known, and he had a great influence on other well-known German composers like George Böhm, Bach and Nicolaus Bruhns.

Johann Fux (1660-1741)

Born of a peasant family in Hirtenfeld, Austria, Fux showed musical talent at an early age, becoming a student at the Jesuit university in Graz in 1680. After studying in Italy, he became court composer to Emperor Leopold I of Austria in 1698, remaining in the imperial service for the rest of his life. His most famous works are the opera, *Constanza e Fortezza* (written to celebrate the coronation of the Emperor Charles VI as king of Bohemia), which received a splendid premier in Prague in 1723, and his *Gradus ad Parnassum* published in 1723. This codified what the age thought to be Palestrina's style in a convenient form for students and nearly every composer from Haydn to Schubert used it as a composition primer.

Felice de Giardini (1716-96)

After being a choirboy at Milan cathedral, Giardini became a member of an opera orchestra in Rome before moving to Naples to direct the Teatro San Carlo orchestra. In 1750 he visited England, where he became a great favourtie, directing the Italian Opera at the King's Theatre and leading the orchestra for the three Choirs Festival from 1770 to 1776. He revisted Naples in 1784, then returned to London in 1790. This time he had little success, and moved to St. Petersburg and then Moscow, where he died in great poverty. He composed attractive chamber music, displaying his gift for melody, and also contributed to English stage works such as *Ruth,* by the English composer Charles Avison.

Michael Haydn (1737-1806)

The younger brother of the famous Joseph Haydn, he became, like him, a choirboy at St. Stephen's Cathedral in Vienna until his voice broke. In 1757 he was made *Kapellmeister* to the Bishop of Grosswardein and in 1763 he became *Konzertmeister* to the Archbishop of Salzburg, in whose service he remained for the rest of his life, succeeeding Mozart as cathedral organist in 1781. He wrote some attractive chamber music and symphonies, though lacked his brother's genius. He is best known for his church music — he composed twenty-four masses, two requiem masses, four German masses as well as operas, oratorios and cantatas — and is particularly well known for his 'Spanish' mass commissioned by the Spanish court in 1786. His pupils included Diabelli and Weber.

Jan Zelenka (1679-1745)

Zelenka began his career as a double bass player at Prague, joining the Dresden royal chapel in 1710. After studying with Fux, he became vice-*Kapellmeister* at Dresden in 1721. His output included about 20 Masses, two *Magnificat* settings, psalms and three oratorios, while his very original instrumental music includes six chamber sonatas, five orchestral capriccios and a chamber concerto. Only recently, when six trio sonatas were resurrected, has he been recognized as a composer of some stature. Some parts of these sonatas have suggested that he was almost as skilled as Bach in the composition of chamber music.

Bibliography

D. Arnold, *Bach* (Past Master Series), Oxford University Press, Oxford, 1984

M. Boyd, *Bach,* J. M. Dent, London, 1983

N. Butterworth, *Haydn: His Life and Times,* Hippocrene Books, New York, 1978

N. Cappell, *Bach the Borrower,* Greenwood Press, Westport, 1980

H. David and A. Mendel, *Bach Reader,* Norton Press, New York, 1972

A. Davidson, *Bach & Handel: The Consummation of the Baroque in Music,* Da Capo, New York, 1986

K. Geiringer, *Haydn: A Creative Life in Music,* University of California Press, Berkeley, 1982

R. Hughes, *Haydn String Quartets,* University of Washington Press, Seattle, 1968

R. Hughes, *Haydn,* J. M. Dent, London, 1978

H. Landon, *Haydn Symphonies,* University of Washington Press, Seattle, 1969

H. Landon (editor), *Haydn Studies,* Norton Press Inc, New York, 1981

C. Millar, *Bach* (Great Master Series), Silver Press, Morristown

J. Pelikan, *Bach Among the Theologians,* Fortress, Philadelphia, 1980

R. Raynor, *Haydn,* Faber and Faber, London, 1972

L. Schraide, *Bach: The Conflict between the Sacred and the Secular,* Da Capo, New York

P. Williams, *Bach Organ Music,* University of Washington Press, Seattle, 1972

P. Williams, *Bach, Handel and Scarlatti: Tercentenary Essays,* Cambridge Univerity Press, Cambridge, 1985

Index